ADDICTION
NATION

TIMOTHY MCMAHAN KING

ADDICTION NATION

What the Opioid Crisis Reveals about Us

HERALD
PRESS

Harrisonburg, Virginia

Herald Press
PO Box 866, Harrisonburg, Virginia 22803
www.HeraldPress.com

Library of Congress Cataloging-in-Publication Data
Names: King, Timothy McMahan, author.
Title: Addiction nation : what the opioid crisis reveals about us / Timothy
    McMahan King.
Description: Harrisonburg, Virginia : Herald Press, 2019. | Includes
    bibliographical references.
Identifiers: LCCN 2019003950| ISBN 9781513804064 (pbk. : alk. paper) | ISBN
    9781513804071 (hardcover : alk. paper) | ISBN 9781513804088 (ebook)
Subjects: LCSH: Opioid abuse--United States. | Opioids--Overdose--United
    States. | Drug abuse--Treatment--United States. | Drug abuse--Social
    aspects--United States.
Classification: LCC RC568.O45 K56 2019 | DDC 362.29/3--dc23 LC record
available at https://lccn.loc.gov/2019003950

Published in association with The Christopher Ferebee Agency,
www.christopherferebee.com.

ADDICTION NATION
© 2019 by Timothy McMahan King
Released by Herald Press, Harrisonburg, Virginia 22803. 800-245-7894.
    All rights reserved.
Library of Congress Control Number: 2019003950
International Standard Book Number: 978-1-5138-0406-4 (paperback);
    978-1-5138-0407-1 (hardcover); 978-1-5138-0408-8 (ebook)
Printed in United States of America
Cover and interior design by Reuben Graham

Portions of chapter 1 first appeared in *Christianity Today*, December 2016.

Portions of chapter 18 first appeared in *Oneing: Perfection 4*, no. 1 (Spring 2016)
published by the Center for Action and Contemplation.

All Scripture quotations, unless otherwise indicated, are quoted, with permission,
from the *New Revised Standard Version*, © 1989, Division of Christian Education
of the National Council of Churches of Christ in the United States of America.

Scripture quotations marked (NIV) are taken from the *Holy Bible, New International Version*®, NIV®. Copyright © 1973, 1978, 1984, 2011 by Biblica, Inc.™
Used by permission of Zondervan. All rights reserved worldwide. www.zondervan
.com The "NIV" and "New International Version" are trademarks registered in
the United States Patent and Trademark Office by Biblica, Inc.™

23 22 21 20 19   10 9 8 7 6 5 4 3 2 1

Contents

1

Beginnings

I don't remember much about the day when everything went wrong. Nothing indicated that a standard outpatient procedure would lead to weeks in the ICU, months in the hospital, and almost a year out of work.

It all started with a routine procedure. I was supposed to be in and out in hours. The doctors, after eliminating the typical causes, were looking for the reason I had developed a mild case of pancreatitis a few weeks before. I didn't know when I left my house that morning how much my life would change. Few people do.

Memories of a dark hospital room and slowly blinking lights come back to me in fevered fits. Dislocated voices from intrusive, floating faces said things would be all right. I had known pain before: crutches, casts, and stitches. But until this moment I had always experienced pain as something outside myself. Now it was all that was left of me.

The day turned into night turned into day turned into night. I had given up on crying for the pain to subside. My soul had turned to the guttural moan of Job. Dear God, if this is my fate, may I never have been born at all.

I heard the words "acute respiratory distress" and was moved to the ICU. I remember how my IV stand became a tree that blossomed with multicolored ornaments hanging from

stainless steel branches. Cascading ripples of wires and tubes
fell to my nose, arms, and chest.

Also hanging there was a clear locked plastic box containing
a small bag marked *hydromorphone*: an opioid pain medication.
The only moment that I remembered I was still a person—that
pain was an experience I was having and not my entire existence—was the moment every fifteen minutes when I pressed
a small button. That button sent a pump whirring and boosted
the slow trickle of that blessed, blessed, blessed analgesic.

Over the course of this medical odyssey, my five-foot, ten-
inch frame dropped below 130 pounds, the whites of my eyes
turned yellow, my stomach distended, and fevers spiked and
dropped. There was vomiting, diarrhea, hallucinations, surgeries, procedures, and minutes turning into hours turning into
days when the doctors would not allow me to place even a
chip of ice in my mouth.

There were crying family members surrounding the hospital bed, desperate phone calls to find a specialist who could
handle my case, and the moment when I heard the doctor say
the words "There is nothing more we can do."

Yet somehow, after weeks in the ICU and months of being
shuttled from hospital to hospital, I was told my situation had
stabilized enough to go home. I was sent home to my apartment
with patches, labeled *fentanyl*, and hydromorphone now in pill
form for the pain. They had inserted a PICC line in the hospital,
a sort of semi-permanent IV line that allowed me to hook up to
a pump for twelve hours a day and receive the liquid and nutrition I needed to survive. A nurse visited twice a week to check
in on me. She cleaned the lines going in and out of my arm, took
blood samples, and made sure I was taking the correct dosage
of the blood thinners I was on to help resolve a blood clot that
had formed during my hospital stay.

Progress was slower than expected. I continued to experience pain when drinking what for most would be a normal

amount of liquid. When I introduced light food, the pain increased, and I'd start vomiting.

During a follow-up appointment with my doctor, he determined that the cause of my ongoing pain and inability to eat was gastroparesis. The pain medicine I had been taking was deadening the nerve endings in my digestive tract and hindering my ability to process food. In other words, the pain medicine was now causing the pain. The more I took to relieve the pain, the more pain I felt.

That's when my doctor told me I had a new and potentially fatal complication: "Tim, you need to know you are addicted to your pain medicine."

My hometown

I didn't see the word *fentanyl* again until I had moved back to my hometown in New Hampshire. It appeared in a local news story. A man had been found dead with a fentanyl patch in his mouth and two more in his stomach.

The fentanyl patches had seemed harmless enough to me, sitting there in a white box next to my bed, in a drawer full of pills, alcohol swabs, and blood thinners. For months they had been a silent presence in my life—attached to my arm, saying nothing, but doing and signifying more than I understood.

That word, *fentanyl*, soon seemed to appear everywhere.

New Hampshire, often tied with Ohio for the second highest drug overdose rates per capita (West Virginia is number one), rose to the top when it came to fentanyl overdoses while I was writing this book. Hillsborough County, where I grew up, is the epicenter. In the time between my release from the hospital and my return to New Hampshire, a period of six years, fentanyl overdoses increased 1,600 percent.

Fentanyl is a synthetic opioid. It is the latest force pushing up overdose rates to new record highs across the United States and Canada. Unlike heroin, you don't need access to a base of opium to make it; you just need the right ingredients. This powerful substance is fifty to one hundred times the strength of heroin; it can be created in a lab by anyone with a basic knowledge of chemistry.

A kilogram of heroin might sell on the street for $60,000, but a kilo of fentanyl can go for $1.3 million.[1] It is so strong that law enforcement officers have nearly died from overdoses through accidental contact and inhalation while making drug arrests.[2] When forty-five kilos were seized from the trunk of a car, experts estimated it was enough to give a fatal dose to every resident of New York City and New Jersey combined.[3] A quarter of a milligram—just a few granules—can be fatal.[4]

Not long ago, a bag of fentanyl powder in New Hampshire dropped below the cost of a six-pack of beer; it is now a common replacement for, or additive to, heroin.[5] Gram for gram, fentanyl is more expensive, but because of its potency, it is far cheaper per dose. I had discovered its power to ease my pain long after other methods had started to lose their effectiveness. Others discovered the same, many at the cost of their lives.

In 1999, I started my freshman year of high school and 8,048 people lost their lives to opioid-related overdoses. In 2009, I was admitted into the hospital and 20,442 people lost their lives to opioid related overdoses. In 2017, the latest data at the time of publication, that number grew to 49,068.[6]

Death rates are highest for thirty-five- to forty-five-year-old white males, with twenty-five- to thirty-four-year-olds of the same demographic following close behind.[7]

I am a white male. I was twenty-five years old when I was sick, and I turned thirty-five the week *Addiction Nation* released.

My story could have had a very different ending.

Why *not* me?

This is not a memoir of extreme addiction or a narrative of personal devastation. I didn't lose my job, destroy relationships, end up in front of a judge, or lose my freedom to incarceration.

I was in the early stages of an opioid addiction, also called a substance use disorder. By diagnostic standards, the addiction was mild. I stood inside the doorway and felt the pernicious chemical grip of opioids. The pills and patches had become more than a treatment for pain. They gave orientation to my life and became the answer to which I turned to relieve anxiety, calm my fear, and give purpose to my days.

My story is one of early detection—of things that went right. It is a story that should be more common than it is. This story isn't so much about who I am or what I did as about what I had—or more accurately, what I had been given. In the end, I had excellent medical care and full insurance coverage. I have a mother who is a nurse, a supportive family, and an upbringing that shielded me from the challenges that many others face. My employer ensured I was financially supported and had a job when I returned. The stigma that so often hangs around the necks of those struggling with addiction was largely absent.

I'm writing this book because if everyone had what I had, the opioid crisis would not be what it is today. Tragically, this is far from the case.

But this is not a memoir, although it does tell parts of my story. Nor is this a self-help book, although I do hope it is helpful. *Addiction Nation* is not a complete history of the opioid crisis or a public policy manifesto, although it will provide insight into both. It is not a scientific analysis or a medical diagnostic manual, but it does try to use these perspectives as tools.

This book is the story of someone who has stood at the edge, who has felt the spiral start, slow, and then stop. It is an exploration of what this crisis says about us, all of us.

I believe the opioid crisis is not an aberrant tragedy or an unexplainable phenomenon, but rather a reflection of ourselves, our culture, our history, our politics, our economy, our materialism. It is about the failures of religion and of an anemic spirituality that we have not wanted to face.

Examining the opioid epidemic, and addiction more broadly, discloses *us* to ourselves. Our desires and excesses, our longings and hidden fears are all on display whether you've ever touched an opioid or not.

The chapters in this book, which are all titled with just one word, join together to do just that. Addiction is more than a *disease*, and the silence and *shame* that has accompanied this epidemic have only shown how deep our struggle with addiction goes. *Blame* aimed at the *other* has failed to address the deep *despair* and *pain* underneath the surface of much of the Western world.

In order to grapple with these overdose deaths, we need better understandings of *sin*, *substances*, and our *bodies*. Our loss of *home*, the changing role of *technology*, and the human desire for *control* have all shaped the way that we experience *choice* in our lives. Our collective *denial* about the extent of our own addictions has meant that we have not yet grappled fully with the loss of *meaning* that plagues so many lives and the tyranny of *perfection* that holds us back from growing into who we are *becoming*.

While the opioid epidemic is new, we can still turn to the old virtues of *faith*, *hope*, and *love* to guide us through. The fact remains that we are all humans in need of *grace* and a new life in *resurrection*. While my own story is present throughout, it is in these final chapters that I begin to unravel some of the new ways I've been able to understand my own experience through my research for this book.

The struggle with addiction is a journey to becoming more fully human. The more we can see ourselves, our connections, and our responsibility for what is happening now, the greater the chance for recovery—for everyone, and not just those struggling with opioids. A society in which those struggling with addiction have the chance to recover isn't just good for those who are addicted; it means greater opportunity for everyone to flourish.

Over the course of my research for this book, I have read books and journal articles, talked with others who have struggled with addiction, and listened to parents who have lost children. I've spoken with public health professionals, therapists, theologians, philosophers, and some of the world's leading experts in addiction studies. I've gone through pages and pages of my own journals and writings from the midst of my own addiction and the early times in my recovery.

This book was not something I expected to write. I used to think of my struggle as simply my own private journey—a story that few would ever need or want to know about. It took me years to understand that my story was not just my own but a window into something much larger.

Addiction Nation is my story. But it is our story too.

A crisis of confidence

The first thing to understand about the opioid crisis is that it is not just about opioids. And, while white men are currently dying at the highest rate, it isn't just about white men.

Instead, it is just the most recent manifestation of a devastating public health crisis of drug overdoses that has been sweeping across the cities, suburbs, and countryside of the United States and Canada for decades. It is born out of a crisis of meaning, a collapse of culture, constant consumption, corporate corruption, the end result of a so-called War on Drugs, a breakdown of public institutions, and a stifling of opportunity.

The story begins in 1979.

On July 15 of that year, President Jimmy Carter addressed the citizens of the United States of America. The president, leading a country just a few years out of the Vietnam War, had planned an address on the ongoing energy crisis, gasoline lines, recession, and rampant inflation. But he changed course because he sensed something more dangerous was at work in the country. It was nearly invisible, Carter said, but it represented a "fundamental threat to American democracy." He called it "a crisis of confidence." We, Carter diagnosed, were losing a confidence in building a future for our children that was better than our own. At the same time, we were losing a connection to the best of our past that could root and ground the country in that vision.

At the heart of the crisis was a question of who we are: "Human identity is no longer defined by what one does, but by what one owns," Carter said. "But we've discovered that owning things and consuming things does not satisfy our longing for meaning. We've learned that piling up material goods cannot fill the emptiness of lives which have no confidence or purpose."

Carter said that the country was faced with two paths. The first reflected the "fragmentation and self-interest" inevitable in a country where people are defined by what they own and consume. In that road, freedom is understood as "the right to grasp for ourselves some advantage over others."

The other path—the one through which he hoped to lead the country—was one of sacrifice, community, and service. "All the traditions of our past, all the lessons of our heritage, all the promises of our future point to another path—the path of common purpose and the restoration of American values," the president said. "That path leads to true freedom for our nation and ourselves."[8]

Carter saw a country that was losing a sense of meaning and purpose. He saw a people with no hope in the future and no lessons and traditions from the past. This is not to romanticize a past that never truly existed but to acknowledge the beginning of an era when a new kind of deadly challenge would spread.

The year 1979 was a turning point for the world's wealthiest nation. That year marked the beginning of the exponential growth of drug overdoses in America. Out of every 100,000 people, 1.13 people died from an accidental drug overdose; in 2016 that number hit 16.96. Every nine years since that speech, drug overdose deaths have doubled, claiming a total of 599,255 lives in that time.[9]

In 2017, drug overdoses once again hit a record high, with over 72,000 lives lost. That's nearly two hundred a day. Most of those deaths are opioid related.

To put these numbers in context, more people died in 2017 from drug overdoses than Americans who died in the entire Vietnam War.

Half of all Americans report knowing someone who has struggled with an opioid addiction. Driven largely by drug overdoses and other "deaths of despair" (more on that in chapter 7), American life expectancy is now set to drop for multiple years in a way not seen for more than a century, when the Spanish flu pandemic claimed the lives of fifty million worldwide.

The path the United States took was not one of shared sacrifice and renewed meaning. The vision that won equated happiness with increased consumption. Pharmaceutical companies promised pain relief without danger. It was a dream of a world that could pursue endless growth without consequence. Meaning and community and sacrifice could take care of themselves—as long as the economy grew.

An ever higher dose of the same approach would temporarily stave off the withdrawal symptoms of the consumerism to which our country was addicted. Few questioned the behaviors that led to the harm in the first place. Those with the most resources have been able to protect themselves the longest. The 1980s ushered in the decade of "greed is good." For some, the economy worked. Many others were left behind.

Marginalized communities, and Black communities in particular, were the first to experience the effects of the crisis. The crack epidemic was an early warning sign that something was wrong. Economically devastated communities—those that had seen economic growth crippled or sabotaged by generations of slavery, debt peonage, and then segregation—were an open wound, one in which the infection of the cheap and hard-hitting drug could spread easily.

Instead of understanding addiction—instead of wondering why so many people would turn to drug use for relief or grasp at low-level dealing as an economic opportunity—we renewed a war on our citizens. Fear of the drug, and an even greater fear of those who were addicted to it, drove the news cycle and won elections. Politicians of both parties stumbled over each other to appear "tough on crime" while failing to address the underlying causes.

Not only did this approach fail; it made the problem worse. The solutions offered lulled the public into a false sense of security that "the problem" had been taken care of, or at least was being managed. All the while, addiction in all forms was growing. The populations who had believed themselves safe were slowly being eroded by the same forces that had hit the most vulnerable communities first.

The failure to address the first wave of this addiction and overdose crisis is now on full and deadly display in white communities across the nation.

If we had learned what we needed to about addiction in the 1980s, we would not be in the situation we are in today. Our failure will likely cost over one million lives to overdoses and the loss of human potential through reckless incarceration of millions more.

We must not fail again.

All are addicts

This story is about us. All of us.

The overdose crisis is just one manifestation of rising addictions across the world. Amid growing wealth, we consume.

With technology designed to connect us, we are isolated. With more to entertain us, satisfy our preferences, and give us everything that we could want, it seems that we have less and less of what we need. Affluence that we hoped would protect us is revealed as a paltry defense from our own insatiable desires.

The greatest mistake we can make is to believe that addiction is "out there" and not our problem. We can read the overdose statistics and feel a sense of sadness but disconnection. Certainly, that could never be *me*, we think; *I* would never let things get that bad or out of control.

"All people are addicts," writes Gerald May in *Addiction and Grace*, reflecting on his long career as a counselor. "Addictions to alcohol and other drugs are simply more obvious and tragic addictions than others have. To be alive is to be addicted, and to be alive and addicted is to stand in need of grace."[10]

In a greater sense, there is no stark designation between those who are addicted and those who are not. Addiction is a spectrum on which we all dwell.

The addictive process is at work in all our lives. Addiction functions in our society and institutions, our politics, and our churches. Addiction feeds an economy and creates jobs even as it destroys lives and communities.

Addiction is present everywhere and every time someone thinks or feels that, as the apostle Paul described, "I do not understand my own actions. For I do not do what I want, but I do the very thing I hate" (Romans 7:15).

Addiction and its devastating consequences are closer than you think.

2

Us

A couple moved in down the street from our family's farm. My brother had gotten to know them when he helped them split enough wood for the winter. They invited him and the rest of my family over for dinner in appreciation.

We made the short walk down the dirt road and were welcomed by two children: a little boy and girl, ages three and six, who were foster children taken in by our neighbors. The siblings had been placed in state custody when their parents robbed the local bank for drug money. The youngest, we learned, refused to sit in his high chair because that was where his parents would leave him for hours, or even days, when they went on drug binges.

The older sister had a face that was somber and aged. Sometimes flashes of laughter or joy made her look like the six-year-old she was, but those sparks always flickered out and her face soon settled back into a world-weary mask more appropriate to a grandmother. Her foster parents explained that she, as a six-year-old, had quickly learned how to take care of herself, her parents, and her younger brother. The instinct to play and laugh had been worn down as she became the responsible party for changing her younger brother and making sure everyone stayed fed.

The Department of Child and Family Services in New Hampshire has been in crisis, as caseloads have spiked along with the opioid epidemic. Caseworkers have been harder to retain, as long hours and continual secondhand trauma burns through staff. It's the same story in departments in other states and Canadian provinces.

What at first surprised and then unsettled me was hearing from our new neighbors how much the birth parents wanted these children back. The parents were now out of prison on bail and awaiting trial. They had gone through treatment and were reportedly no longer using. Our neighbors let us know to be on the lookout for suspicious activity because, while the parents had limited visitation rights, they had asked for full custody and been denied by the court. They were upset and had made threats that they would take their children back by force if need be.

We all struggled to see the remains of what must have once been, and maybe still was, parental love. Our neighbors knew that the children's birth parents felt genuine care and concern for their children. At the same time, the foster parents found it impossible to forgive, and difficult to even look into the eyes of those who had so abused and mistreated these children whom they had come to care for so much in just a few months.

I don't know the rest of the story of those children, or what happened to their birth parents. It's not unusual to get only short glimpses—snippets of the lives of those addicted to opioids and the pain and trauma in their wake. I walked away from my neighbors' house that evening with a mixture of sadness, disgust, and anger.

How could anyone treat these children—or any child, for that matter—the way these kids had been treated? I hoped for them what I would hope for every child: a safe, loving, and stable home. That they might have a chance to grow and thrive and that the lives of the parents would not forever mark the lives of the children.

Our farm had always seemed insulated from the world by the trees and fields that surrounded it. "Real drug problems" were in cities like New York, Baltimore, Chicago, and Los Angeles. If my neighbors ever used drugs, we would have called it "experimentation" or "recreational use," not the crime and trafficking of the cities. That night cracked the protective glass I had erected around my vision of a quaint hometown in a wholesome state. It revealed more lingering biases then I am comfortable to admit.

A hidden fear

The line between me and those parents is thinner than I like to think. Lots of lines—between tragedy and redemption, sinner and saint, addiction and faith, healing and harm—seem so thin, so translucent, that they almost don't exist.

Like many encounters with human pain and suffering, this one brought with it a stirring of guilt—a weight born of proximity to crisis. Sometimes those emotions are hidden, and other times they are well surfaced. Sometimes we feel guilty because of our own incapacity to step in and stop the suffering. Other times guilt comes brushed with a stroke of complicity—that feeling of responsibility for simply being the same species as someone who acted in such a way. If the same capacity resides in another human, it may reside in us as well. If we can't stop the pain, we are implicated by its perpetuation.

Those parents could not just be reduced to isolated bad actors who could be cast out or punished to fix whatever was wrong. They pointed to a crisis, one that I had felt the pull of before.

I remember the warm wrap of opioids that kept me in my bed with my chin on my chest. My movements slowed and disconnected, I had become an observer of my own body, with control so far lost it seemed only a memory. My vision became so narrowed that I saw no other choice except one pill or two or three.

I remember the strange, soothing voice in my head reminding me that the only sure protection from pain so intense that I had prayed for my own existence to be blotted out was found in the bottle of pills beside me. It was that voice that I trusted and which made it so hard to hear anything else.

Philosopher Francis Seeburger writes, "At least part of what makes us react with such abhorrence to images of the depths of addiction, refusing to admit any community with addicts who have plumbed those depths, is our hidden fear that we are like them."[1] We are afraid because we are all closer than we would ever want to admit. The lines I had drawn between my hometown and the rest of the world weren't just a little off; they were lies, signs of denial.

The discomfort I felt as I left our neighbors' house was not the result of distance but of connection, not of difference but of sameness. Something inside me knows that I, too, am capable of neglect and cruelty. I, too, have done, said, and thought things that I don't want to think myself capable of doing, saying, or thinking. I have been quick to protest, "But I am not that kind of person!"

But we protest too much. We might even believe our own denials—until that moment the rooster crows for the third time and the sun comes up to reveal the truth we had hoped to avoid.

All of us have acted in ways or said things that we later regret. We have all convinced ourselves that something was okay—only to later feel a sense of guilt because, deep inside, we knew it was wrong all along. Time after time, we have set out to accomplish a goal or to change a behavior with the best of intentions only to find ourselves failing. The "I could never . . ." or "I would never . . ." or "I just can't imagine how . . .": all mask a deep fear rooted in the knowledge that we, too, have felt out of control. When we encounter stories of addiction, in some way we encounter ourselves. When we see others trapped in addiction, reflected back are so many things we would rather not admit about our own lives.

Terence, the enslaved Roman playwright, wrote, "I am human, and I consider nothing that is human alien to me." It is true of the good and the bad, the ugly and the beautiful, the triumph and the failure.

To struggle with control of our own actions is at the heart of what it means to be human. Addiction is just one of the most obvious ways that this challenge manifests.

How we define

The work of defining and understanding addiction is critical. Precision in our language matters. At the same time, we also can come to understand addiction through our own connection and shared experiences.

A friend who tells you "Watch out—that cat is about to pounce!" could be technically correct when describing a tabby kitten about to jump on your shoulder . . . or a bobcat about to jump out of a tree and onto your head. Both creatures are cats. But delineating between the two could be a matter of life and death.

When you want to define a term, one approach is to get specific. You can define a tree by determining if it is evergreen with needles, or maybe it is deciduous and loses its leaves every year. You can check how many leaves are on a stem, the shape of the leaves and the color and texture of the bark. Eventually, you can identify that it isn't just a hardwood but a maple, and not just a maple but a sugar maple.

These sorts of definitions are important, especially in scientific research (or when dodging a bobcat attack). Specificity is one approach to defining something: this is what a maple is, and this is what it is not. The lines are clear.

But that isn't the only way we define things—not even trees. We can also identify a tree by what it is near, or as the place where you built a childhood treehouse. If you want someone to understand the first tree you ever climbed, you don't give family, genus, species, and variety. You tell the story of what that tree means to you and how you are connected to it.

You learn a whole lot more about a tree on my parents' property, and about who I am, when you learn that maple syrup has been made on my family's farm for hundreds of years, and that my mom kept my third-grade science project where I tested how many gallons of sap it takes to make a gallon of maple syrup (about forty gallons, in case you are wondering). To define that maple tree in the front yard, I could tell you that I used to climb it while wearing a homemade cape to read *The Hobbit* in its branches.

You can learn a lot about a person by knowing their Social Security number, address, credit score, and a full map of their genome. But there is a whole world to explore—a whole definition to emerge—when we hear about their likes, dislikes, stories, friends, family, passions, and loves.

The way we describe a thing, experience, or person doesn't just reveal something about what we are trying to describe; it reveals something about the one who is doing the describing. Our choice of description, and even definition, tells us about the describer.

Say you ask a friend about the person they just went on a first date with. If you get a vague physical description, their hometown, and the general impression that they have a good credit score, your friend has "defined" their date with good, specific information. You also know things might not work out.

But if your friend uses the language of connection—how they found the other person so attractive, how they enjoy hearing the other person laugh, seeing their smile, and listening to their stories—well, you know that they are probably going to see each other again real soon.

We can define things—cats, trees, a person's theology, a nation's epidemic—by getting specific and granular. Or we can define them by what they mean to us and how we are connected to them. Both matter.

When it comes to addiction, understanding the definitions that emerge from neuroscience, biochemistry, psychology, physiology, sociology, public policy, and economics is critical. But far too often we read the stories of addiction in the newspaper, see them on television, or hear about them from our neighbor, and our instinct is to distance ourselves from those who are addicted. We create definitions that separate ourselves from "addicts." We use a precision of language to protect and insulate ourselves from the pain we might feel if we ourselves are implicated. We begin to feel self-righteous, a sense that may justify a lack of personal engagement or punitive public policy.

But what if we defined addiction not by drawing lines around it, as in "This is what addiction is; this is what it is not"? What if we defined addiction by drawing out our connections?

"I am not being flippant when I say that all of us suffer from addiction," writes Gerald May. "Nor am I reducing the meaning of addiction. I mean in all truth that the psychological, neurological, and spiritual dynamics of full-fledged addiction are actively at work within every human being."[2]

The question for each of us is not *whether* we are addicted but *how* we are addicted, and to *what*. Denial of the existence of addiction in your life is not a mark of moral accomplishment but a sign of blindness.

Defining addiction by the facts and the figures of a particular epidemic is crucial for helping us understand the magnitude of what we're facing. But defining addiction by the way

in which it touches all of us—even resides within us—helps us
see it in a whole new light.

Our addictive existence

Peg O'Connor, a philosopher writing from her own experience
with addiction says, "Questions about addictions are, at rock
bottom, questions about the meaning of life."[3] Most medical
and psychological research focuses on addiction as an aberra-
tion, a disorder, and a malfunction. But what if addiction also
reveals something about our culture, our economy, and our
world that is very much considered "normal" but is actually
destroying what is human? How can we understand addiction
in a way that gives insight and speaks truth to the entirety of
our existence?

Maybe addiction is a force so pervasive in our culture—
so supported by our economy and defining of our human
predicament—that we all are vulnerable to it. Maybe we are
born into a flowing stream that, unless we actively choose
otherwise, will draw us into a flow of addiction. Philosopher
Frank Schalow writes that when he uses the word *addiction*,
he does not mean "a clinical or medical diagnosis concerning
a person's dependence on a specific substance, e.g., drugs or
alcohol." Rather, he writes, addiction refers to "a broader his-
torical and cultural transformation of our way 'to be' (as well
as an individually based problem). Could it be the case that
addiction is a harbinger of shifting cultural horizons, and is as
much emblematic of an impending (human) crisis as a whole,
rather than only a medical or clinical problem?"[4]

I'm addicted. So are you. That's okay.

It's not okay because our addictions are not harmful or
damaging. It is not okay because they do not denigrate ourselves and others and close us off from the world. It is not
okay because they do not cut us off from our freedom, our
identity, and the core of what it means to be fully human.

Rather, it's okay because we are in this together. This common struggle should bind us together as we face a common fate. The more categories we create between deserving and undeserving, sympathetic and irredeemable, the greater danger we run of failing to understand addiction altogether.

A person struggling with an opioid addiction faces challenges that are, at root, the challenges we all face. The world in which we find ourselves is one whose center of gravity pulls us down into our own addictive capacities.

Addiction is a word used so often and in such varied contexts that our assumptions about its meaning become something of a Rorschach test. I assumed I knew what addiction was until the day my doctor told me I was addicted. I did not realize at the time how much unlearning I would have to do.

3

Disease

It was more than five years before I talked with anyone who wasn't in that doctor's office or part of my medical team about being addicted to opioids.

My mother had been in the room with me that day the doctor told me that I was addicted. She had flown from New Hampshire to Washington, D.C., to be at that follow-up appointment. As we drove away, we talked about what the doctor had just said. "It makes sense," she said with relief.

After so many medical complications and close calls, the ongoing mystery of what had been slowing my recovery was a burden. The assurance of a path forward was greater than the weight of what that path was. As a nurse, my mother had seen both the necessity of the medicine and the dangers it carried. She understood that what had previously been life-giving was now numbing my digestive system, increasing my sensitivity to pain, and causing physical dependence.

In those days, my mother and I talked about what was next. We talked about the ways my body still hurt and the ways it was healing. We talked about the steps forward, and we talked about the steps back. We talked about when the pain got worse and when the pain got better.

We talked about the nutrition pumped from a clear plastic bag straight into my bloodstream. We talked about the blood thinners I was on and the blood clots they protected me from. We talked about moving on from clear liquids. We talked about the broth I sipped, then the white rice I ate, and then the baby food that would be best for me to try first.

We talked about the few weeks I stopped taking pain medicine entirely. We talked about the solid foods I began to eat.

We talked about when I went back into the emergency room late one night when the pain returned. We talked about the week I spent in the hospital and about which surgeon should perform the surgery to remove my gallbladder. We talked about getting better and the pain medicine I was on again.

We talked about every aspect of my hospital stay. We talked about every part of my recovery. We could talk about everything but addiction.

I don't think either of us even knew where to start.

Rise of the disease model

We hear the word *addiction* all the time. Coffee, chocolate, and social media are all called addictive. Companies proudly market their products' addictive qualities, claiming that potential users won't be able to stop once they've begun.

In 2011, a year after that meeting with my doctor, America's largest professional association of doctors working to treat and prevent addiction adopted a new definition of addiction. Addiction is "a primary, chronic disease of brain reward, motivation, memory and related circuitry," the physicians of the American Society of Addiction Medicine (ASAM) said. "Dysfunction in these circuits leads to characteristic biological, psychological, social and spiritual manifestations. This is reflected in an individual pathologically pursuing reward and/or relief by substance use and other behaviors."[1]

Addiction as a disease: the idea was not a new one, but in the medical world this marked a significant shift that had been underway for decades. The "decade of the brain" in the 1990s led to burgeoning neuroscientific research that narrowed in on the many ways that addiction damages tissue and creates dysfunction in the brain.

Not long ago, addiction was understood primarily as a result of poor moral choices. This is often referred to as the "moral model" of addiction. This perspective suggests that it is a lack of self-control, discipline, honesty, and self-understanding that leads some to become addicted. Addiction was seen as a symptom of underlying moral depravity and maladjustment.

Caroline Jean Acker, in her book *Creating the American Junkie*, tells the story of Dr. Lawrence Kolb, the first medical director of the Federal Narcotic Hospital. A series of papers he published in 1925 outlined the moral model that would dominate medical, governmental, and public understanding of addiction for decades to come. While Kolb would spend the later years of his life working to undo the harm these ideas created, their impact is still felt today.[2]

Kolb argued that while a few "innocent" addicts might have become addicted through a prescription from their doctors, those instances were rare. Those who did get addicted were mostly "psychopaths" or "psychoneurotics," he said, who displayed these behavioral problems and character deficiencies well before they ever became addicted.

The problem of those addicted stemmed primarily from their "defective personalities," Kolb claimed, and manifested in a refusal to conform to societal norms. The solution? Quarantine them in an asylum or incarcerate them. Addiction was a deviance, and it was presented as just one of the many moral failings of the person who was addicted.

The rise of the disease model represented a dramatic shift from this approach. It is not that those without self-control became addicts, this perspective argues, but that the addiction could cause the lack of self-control. If a person who is addicted lies, cheats, or steals, it is not because they have always been the kind of person who lies, cheats, or steals; it is the addiction itself that causes the behavior.

In the press release announcing the new definition of addiction, Raju Hajela, past president of the Canadian Society of Addiction Medicine and chair of the ASAM committee that developed the new definition, stated, "The disease creates distortions in thinking, feelings and perceptions, which drive people to behave in ways that are not understandable to others around them. Simply put, addiction is not a choice. Addictive behaviors are a manifestation of the disease, not a cause."[3]

Addiction is often compared to type 2 diabetes or heart disease. Different people, because of their genes, have different likelihoods of getting the disease. Lifestyle factors matter. Individual choices matter. But lifestyle factors and choices are not the only factors in determining whether someone develops the disease.

When it comes to treatment of diabetes, exercise and change in diet are critical, but so are medications and other medical supports. A pep talk to your pancreas isn't going to help your body regulate blood sugar, and an inspirational book doesn't unclog a blocked artery.

"Many chronic diseases require behavioral choices, such as people with heart disease choosing to eat healthier or begin exercising, in addition to medical or surgical interventions," said Dr. Michael Miller, past president of ASAM and the one who oversaw the change in definition. "We have to stop moralizing, blaming, controlling or smirking at the person with the disease of addiction, and start creating opportunities for individuals and families to get help and providing assistance in choosing proper treatment."[4]

The disease model of understanding addiction has been an important advancement in addiction science. It has become the dominant model of understanding addiction, creating a framework for how to treat it and a driving force in providing new modes of approaching it from the public policy perspective. It also isn't the entire story.

End of the moral model

In my recovery, the idea of addiction as a disease allowed me to let down my defenses and accept help. What I needed to understand was the physiological and medical aspects of the changes that months of heavy opioid use, and my eventual addiction, had made in my brain.

My doctor told me something that day that was critical for me to hear: "You need to know this is not your fault," he said. "You didn't do anything wrong. You needed the pain medicine, and we gave it to you. Your body was in so much stress from the pain it could have triggered more complications and you might not have made it otherwise."

I don't know if I would have admitted it at the time, but deeply ingrained in my brain was the belief that "addicts" are bad and weak-willed. They lack discipline and self-control. They can't handle pain and only live for a selfish pursuit of pleasure. So what my doctor said disrupted me from that well-worn track. It opened me up to a different way of understanding both addiction and myself.

But the disease model isn't the only way to understand addiction. In fact, there are limitations.

At least one study shows that alcoholics who believe that their alcoholism is a disease are more likely to relapse than those who don't.[5] Why? Thinking you have a disease can lead some people to believe that the responsibility of a cure, of healing, belongs to a doctor or medical professional. This is a problem with treating not just addiction but other diseases, like type 2 diabetes and heart disease, as well.

Models are not always right or wrong. Instead, they vary in how helpful, or harmful, they can be in helping us understand a complex phenomenon. Newton created a scientific model that helped us understand a lot about the world. When Einstein came along, he developed an even better and more accurate model. Since then, physicists have improved on Einstein. Not everything Newton or Einstein discovered suddenly became wrong, but we did learn that an apple falling from a tree was a lot more complicated than it initially looked.

There are other limitations to the disease model, as we'll see later, but that doesn't mean it needs to be thrown out entirely. The disease model has brought dramatic leaps forward in understanding the effects of addiction on the brain and in developing new therapies and drugs to address these changes. With the disease model, and any model of addiction, we need to appreciate what it illuminates and to be aware of what it might cover up.

Addiction is complex. The overdose crisis is complex. There are many windows to look through to try and understand. Here are just a few of them.

The physicians at ASAM see the primary frame as medical. They would say I showed early signs of a chronic disease that had altered the structure of my brain. The nature of the disease was such that I was unable to see my own symptoms, and I would need treatment from medical professionals in order to recover. A step-down program off my existing medication could be supplemented with alternative non-opioid pain medicine and other medication that could reduce cravings and help my body adjust.

Some scientists would look at the systems of the body at work and understand what adaptive purposes addiction-like behaviors might have served in our past. An evolutionary biologist would be particularly curious about the genetic or epigenetic factors at play.

In Alcoholics Anonymous, there is a spiritual story at work. The hope for those with an addiction comes in a moment of spiritual clarity that reorients a person's life to see the way in which they are powerless over their addiction. The disease of addiction can be overcome by acknowledging a "higher power" and its role in one's recovery.

Psychologists would call it a substance use disorder. Not so much a disease, as if it were caused by a foreign pathogen, but still a disruption of normal cognitive functioning. They might see a need for medication, but would also focus on a variety of therapies. Some might be interested in what wounds or defense mechanisms I developed in the past and need to relearn in order to address the addiction. Others would be focused on my future, how to help me accomplish my goals through changing my perspective and teaching me new strategies for behavioral modification.

Still others might be more focused on the social factors of my life. Do I have a job to return to? A home that I can go to? Friends whom I can talk to? Will I return to an environment in which addiction to opioids or other substances is a norm? Do I have a community that provides meaning and direction and support for my recovery?

Economists might note the increasing potency of the opioids available for decreasing costs, or they might critique the cost-saving incentives enacted by insurance companies that cover opioids for long-term and chronic pain but don't cover more expensive but holistic methods of pain management. They might also note that an efficient distribution system of illicit substances almost always requires a level of income inequality, and that you need people with the resources to buy the substance and those with few resources and desperate situations willing to take the risk of selling them.

Public policy experts would note that current regulations don't discourage large pharmaceutical companies from deceptive practices. Any fines for deceiving the public are only a small percentage of the total profits made through the deception. Or they might note how private prisons lobby for and politicians enact policies that are seemingly "tough on crime" but not only are less effective at treating addiction than known alternatives but actively create a context where addiction will thrive.

Theologians might be compelled by the ways addiction resembles a kind of worship or how addiction can sometimes feel like a battle raging for our souls. Philosophers might be intrigued by the way that addiction does not seem to be a simple behavior like walking or running but a way of being, a totalizing means of describing one's existence.

This is just a short list of possible frameworks by which to view addiction, its causes, and the environments where it thrives. None of these perspectives are wrong. In understanding not just my situation but the crisis we find ourselves in, each one is important, and none of them are complete. There is no one simple cause of the crisis we are in and there will be no singular solution.

Understanding the opioid crisis requires experts who make breakthroughs within their fields. But it also requires exploring the connections between these fields and linking those discoveries back to our lived experience.

Wilberforce

Rejecting the moral model of addiction, which suggests that addicts are just weak-willed sinners, does not mean that every other model has nothing to do with morality. It is an acknowledgment that the moral model represented a bad understanding of morality.

The moral model is the equivalent of the geocentric view of the universe. Yes, we can understand why observers in the past believed that the sun revolved around the earth; it was an easy explanation. But just as we now know that the sun does not revolve around the earth, we also know that those who are addicted are not a distinct class of immoral people. The moral model persists, however, and it inhibits progress. Part of its persistence resides in how easy it is to believe, especially for those in the middle of the struggle, who then blame themselves and give up hope that they can change.

One story that helped break me out of that well-worn rut of moral assumptions and self-blame is the inspiring story of one of the world's great abolitionists, William Wilberforce. His story is quite well known. Born in 1759, the son of a wealthy trader, Wilberforce eventually became a politician in Great Britain.

His early years as a legislator were unremarkable, and he said of himself, "The first years in Parliament I did nothing— nothing to any purpose. My own distinction was my darling object."[6]

After a spiritual experience on Easter of 1786, his life changed. He abstained from alcohol and practiced rigorous self-examination as befit, he believed, a "serious" Christian. He founded the Society for the Suppression of Vice, whose mission was "the encouragement of piety and virtue; and . . . the preventing of vice, profaneness, and immorality."[7]

One of Wilberforce's main causes was the abolition of the slave trade. For eighteen years he worked to end the practice. Each year he was thwarted by vested interests and the status quo. He was attacked publicly and ridiculed by many of his peers for trying to upend what was considered a bedrock institution of society.

His tireless commitment, even amid declining health, has served as an inspiration for the world. He never gave up hope, and persevered despite the personal toll and sacrifice. While he was not present for the final vote, he learned just three days before his death that passage of an abolition act was assured. He died knowing that the slave trade in Great Britain would finally end.

The entanglement he was never able to defeat, however, was his own thirty-year opium addiction. He began taking the

drug as a medicine for ongoing ill health. His dosage continued to increase, and even though he tried, he was never able
to quit. Wilberforce died of a respiratory disease, which was
likely hastened by his heavy use of opium.

At the time, the word *addiction* was not yet used to describe
alcohol or drug use. One early use of the word *addicted* was
a passage in the King James translation of the Bible in 1
Corinthians where the translator describes a family that has
"addicted themselves to the ministry of the saints."

The word addict at the time, was a verb and not a noun. It
was "to devote or give up (oneself) to a habit or occupation."[8]
Daily use, combined with harmful results for one's health and
well-being, would certainly count as addiction by today's standards. But if Wilberforce had been described by his peers to be
addicted to anything, it would have been the elimination of
the slave trade.

Addiction is not caused by immorality, nor does it necessarily cause immorality. Wilberforce both lived a life of great
moral accomplishment and struggled for decades with an opioid addiction.

If opioid addiction had the same stigma back then that it
does today, we might never have known the name William
Wilberforce.

Shame, silence, and stigma have made this epidemic the
deadly force that it is today.

4

Shame

The newspaper editors were surprised when Robert submitted his son's obituary. Most people in this situation, they explained, don't mention the cause of death. Or if they do, they use vague phrases such as "died of complications" or "died suddenly."

December 18 changed everything for Robert's family. That morning a father found his son barely breathing, just a few weeks after coming home from rehab. A few years earlier, the young man had been an athlete and honors student, known as a good kid from a good home. A broken arm had led to a prescription for Percocet, had led to buying pills, had led to heroin.

The son got help. He knew he needed it. After a seemingly successful stint in rehab, he had gone back to his father's home for the holidays. A dealer was waiting. He began texting Robert's son as soon as he returned. The dealer was trying to keep up his own habit, and reconnecting with an "old friend" was his way to do it.

It didn't take much. Robert's son took the dose he had been taking before rehab. He didn't factor in the decreased tolerance that sobriety had brought.

His father found him with the needle still in his arm. He held his son during those final breaths, the ambulance on its way. Robert was there when he heard the paramedics say it was too late. There was nothing more to be done.

Robert had been an involved and caring father, and he didn't know what more he could have done. Few parents do. Thomas McLellan, a leading addiction researcher, admitted that when he discovered his own son was wrestling with addiction, he didn't know what to do or how to find help.

But Robert knew his first step. No, Robert explained to the newspaper editor, he would not use a euphemism. He would publish the actual nature of his son's death. His son, he explained, was not a moral degenerate. He had never stopped being a good kid, never stopped having potential and the opportunity for a bright future.

His son was the victim of an epidemic that thrived, in part, from the way it could stay hidden in the shadow of shame. Shame hung around the necks of those who suffered the most. Shame prevented families from including the true cause of death in their children's obituaries, and shame meant that each family's sorrow was held closely and guarded from the outside world.

Shame has not just been a result of this crisis; it has fueled it.

Silence

Dreamland by Sam Quinones and *Dopesick* by Beth Macy both detail the rise of the opioid epidemic in the United States. The books tell different stories, each tracing a distinct path the epidemic has taken, but binding them together are the compelling topics of silence and shame.

Quinones describes how his reporting started with public officials and law enforcement. When he turned his attention to parents who had chosen to publicly fight the epidemic after their own losses, he wrote that he could find only a few; "most grieving families retreated in shame and never said a public word about how a son died in a halfway house with a needle in his arm."[1]

Quinones began reporting on the crisis in the mid-2000s, when opioid-related overdoses were at 16,000 per year. By 2008, drug overdoses as a whole would overtake car crashes as the leading cause of accidental death in the United States. Today, even those numbers look tame. The rate of death was unlike any the country had seen before, even as the attention the issue received was minimal. This was, in part, because the very people who would normally raise the alarm and demand action—those closest to the crisis—were keeping the true cause of their pain hidden.

Macy, who published her book a few years later, describes this silence as an exacerbating factor of an already danger- ous situation. "Prescription pill and heroin abuse was allowed to fester, moving quietly and stealthily across this country, cloaked in stigma and shame," she writes.[2] Macy describes small groups of parents, mostly mothers, who began find- ing each other, commiserating and consoling each other in living rooms and funeral homes. One woman who publicly acknowledged the cause of her son's death owned a jewelry store in Virginia. She quickly learned to spot the parents who would come into her store, pretend to browse for a few min- utes, and then quietly approach her to say that their child was addicted, and they didn't know what to do. Parents would only speak out, Macy writes, when they decided "that survival had to trump shame."[3]

Janine, who lost her son Bobby to an overdose, had worked in her community to start the Hope Initiative, a group that provides information about addiction and connections to a variety of treatment options. She had thought that the local school board in her district, where the high school was full of struggling students seeking help, might provide some support.

Janine went to a meeting of that school board to share the story of her son's death, hoping that the high school might collaborate with the Hope Initiative as a way to support the increasing number of students struggling with addiction. She shared how she had done everything she could to get her children into this school district because she believed it was a better place to raise her children than in some of the surrounding communities, which were economically depressed. But now, crime statistics indicated, things were actually worse in the wealthier community where they had settled. "The affluence she believed would protect her family had instead allowed the festering of shame and inaction," writes Macy.[4]

The school board declined to give any funding to the program. In talking with parent advocates, Macy found that the story of a community's denial was not unique. Giving money, time, effort, and attention to a solution means first admitting that there is a problem.

Imagine being a high school principal in a community in which opioid use and overdoses are growing. The first child dies, and the parents ask for privacy. You understand and respect the request. But the deaths continue. You know it is a problem not just in your school but in the entire region. Yet you also know that the moment you would start a program related to addiction, all the public attention would zero in on your school. If no other schools in the area address the crisis, it would look as if something is wrong with your school. Parents who used to feel safe sending their children there would suddenly become worried. Residents would begin to move away to other school districts, and your district would lose funding. So maybe you hope the opioid wave will affect just a few kids, and that it will quickly pass.

It is not hard to see how thousands of small actions intended to protect individuals, families, and communities have perpetuated a deadly silence. The shame experienced in the midst of loss has made it harder for those who need support to find each other. The belief that addiction is somehow a unique failure—of their own children and of their entire family—has kept many parents from speaking out about addiction as the public health crisis that it is.

But silence isn't always the result of remaining quiet. It also comes in the form of being silenced. When it came to the rise of crack cocaine in communities of color, the dominant story told was of "superpredators," "welfare queens," and "crack babies." The voices that told a story of failing schools, few jobs, and counterproductive law enforcement strategies were drowned out. This silencing can lead to an internalization of the lies themselves.

"What are the words you do not yet have?" writes philosopher and poet Audre Lorde. "What do you need to say? What are the tyrannies you swallow day by day and attempt to make your own, until you sicken and die of them, still in silence?"[5]

Hiddenness

Just as shame keeps quiet the families of those who have lost loved ones to drug overdoses, shame keeps quiet those who struggle with addiction themselves.

When Adam and Eve ate of the fruit in the garden, the first thing they did was hide themselves from each other. "The eyes of both were opened, and they knew that they were naked; and they sewed fig leaves together and made loincloths for themselves" (Genesis 3:7). The second thing they did? Hide from God. "They heard the sound of the Lord God walking in the garden at the time of the evening breeze, and the man and his wife hid themselves from the presence of the Lord God among the trees of the garden" (verse 8).

Shame is at the heart of the way we deceive ourselves and others. Shame is what tells us to cover up and hide. It is what tells us to cut off our connection to others and avoid their knowing gaze. Shame is a warning sign that we feel as our throats narrow and stomachs tighten with that full-body knowledge that something is not right.

In *Being and Nothingness*, French philosopher Jean-Paul Sartre describes looking through a keyhole. He is spying on another person and completely engrossed in his task. He hears the footsteps of another person and realizes that he, too, is being watched.

Sartre feels a sense of shame roll over him, he writes. He realizes that another person is observing him. This person doesn't see all of who he is, but merely the part of himself involved in the shameful action of spying.

In this scenario, a few things are happening at once. First, Sartre realizes he is doing something wrong: he is spying on someone. Instead of treating whomever he is spying on as a person like himself, deserving of dignity, respect, and privacy, he reduces the person to the object of his gaze.

Second, he realizes that the same thing is happening to him. Another person has just seen him spying, and instead of seeing all of Sartre, they also reduce *him* to an object of their gaze. They see him not as a person but as a spy.

We experience shame when another person observes us in a state of, as Sartre would say, "being as we are not." We engage in an action, and someone sees it. We become aware of the way that we are being seen, but also all the ways that we are *not* being seen. We react to shame with a desire to run after the person, shouting, "But wait! Let me explain."

When I first considered writing about my own struggle, this was what I felt. I was concerned that if I published my story, then I would become an Addict in the eyes of others. Readers would not see me or the fullness of who I am, but I would be reduced to that guy who wrote about his addiction to pain medicine.

Addictions thrive amid shame because we remove ourselves from others in the exact moments that we most need help and connection. Our instinct is to throw on a couple of fig leaves and join Adam and Eve in the bushes. The worry that someone might think we are addicted can drive us to hide the addictive behavior, and in the shadows it grows.

I didn't speak of my addiction for years in the belief that it was a private struggle, not noteworthy or of interest or meaning to anyone but myself. Parents silently hold the pain of watching a child slip away, not knowing their neighbors just down the street are also crying. The voices of communities of color are drowned out by the sensationalized images of young men in handcuffs so that politicians can say they were "doing something" about violence and crime on the street.

Shame, like the addictions it feeds, isn't easy to erase.

Just say no?

The genesis of *Addiction Nation* was a piece I wrote for *Christianity Today*. Authors don't often have input into the titles of their pieces. In this case, the editors decided to title my article "Just Say No to Shame," to play off my critique of the "Just say no" anti-drug campaigns of the 1980s and 1990s.

The editors' thinking was clear. In a piece about the negative aspects of shame, "just saying no to shame" is a clever twist to encourage readers to find freedom from their own shame. Shame, in its own way, can be an addicting, damaging, and paralyzing force.

But it isn't a good idea to "just say no to shame." Shame, like many other negative feelings, grows and thrives when it is denied. When we deny that we feel shame, we can begin to feel shame that we don't feel shame. Or if we press down the shame, it bides its time beneath the surface and manifests in other ways. Soon we might even begin acting in ways that we don't want to in order to prove to ourselves that we don't feel shame. We exaggerate our own behaviors and beliefs in unnatural ways in order to declare that we will not be controlled by shame.

But in this case, shame hasn't lost control; it has only changed its manifestation. Shame remains in charge, but now in a hidden way. We think we are freely choosing our own actions when in fact we are acting the way we are because of the shame that we feel.

I would not be surprised if at least a part of our political leaders' failure to respond is a result of unrealized shame. They feel shame at their own ineffectiveness, and instead of doing the long and hard work of addressing the root causes of addiction, which might make them look "weak" or "soft," they punish the symptoms of addiction by being "tough on crime."

The actions might be different, but they still arise from shame. They still come from the same place. We can assume a new identity or take on a different persona to try to press down the shame, but we still aren't free. In fact, the chains have been strengthened. No chains are as strong as the ones we convince ourselves don't exist.

Shame, when it first pops up, isn't necessarily a bad thing. It is the alarm bell that someone is seeing us act in a way that we want to make sure doesn't define us. It can begin in a place of warning—a sense that we have violated our own moral compass.

But shame quickly blossoms out of control. And because shame is always related to being seen, our sense of shame may or may not come from whether something is right or wrong. It could very well come from a belief we've internalized from society, family, or our religious upbringing.

These complicated origins of shame mean that one of our greatest challenges is understanding our shame, not saying no to it. We need to untangle the web of our emotions, not simply say no to them. The sense of shame I felt as I walked back down the dirt road after that visit with my neighbors was a feeling not to be ignored but to be unpacked, understood, and learned from.

Shame is not just an emotional reflex; it is tied into what we believe to be true about ourselves, others, and the world around us. We need to dive into the motivations and beliefs, both hidden and on the surface, to understand the origins of our shame.

The problem isn't that shame becomes present; the problem occurs when shame is in control. The problem isn't that we ever feel shame; it is that we begin to believe the lies that shame will inevitably tell if we allow it to stay.

Shame succeeds when it overwhelms us and withers when it is understood and brought back into its place. Shame never has more power than when it is hidden. And while exposing it might be painful, the pain is the final feeling before being relieved of those chains.

What does it look like to create a culture where Robert and Janine are not lone voices crying in the wilderness but leading voices in communities of support and understanding? What if their children, and the children of so many others, did not feel they needed to hide their pain and struggles in the shadows but could speak out and say they need help?

Shame can be a death sentence, but it doesn't have to be.

5

Blame

"You need to come in for a drug test. We think you are abusing your pain medicine."

"You don't really need that much pain medicine at this point. You are about to be discharged and you need to figure out how to deal without it."

"Ma'am, you need to understand. We think your son is just putting on a show for his mother. At this point, he's just looking for pain medicine."

I had a lot of different doctors over the course of my medical journey, and multiple hospital transfers. Three separate times I was told, or my mother was told, that I was faking my pain in order to get more narcotics. Such suspicion is not surprising. My younger sister, Abby, works as an emergency room nurse and has to discern on every shift how to respond to suspicious stories, especially from "frequent fliers," who return every few days in search of more drugs. My story, she admits, would be suspicious if she didn't know me personally. In my case, each time the doctors missed a complication that would later reveal itself. Each time I felt the need to justify my need for the drugs by proving the depth of my pain to both myself and others. The more I felt that need, the more I felt the pain.

Given all the suspicion and the constant feeling of having to prove my pain, the day my doctor told me that I was addicted to opioids, I was ready to fight. I thought I would hear once again that it was my fault, that I was to blame. I tensed up as I got ready to hear that I was faking it, that I had done something wrong. I realize now that I was ready to go on the defensive before the doctor even opened his mouth that day.

These drugs had finally offered me a sense of relief and safety. They had given me something I needed for my life and my health. I had been in acute respiratory distress with a fear of multiple organ systems failing, so the added stress of severe pain was not just uncomfortable but potentially deadly. The feeling the pain medicine gave was of ongoing protection. When someone questioned whether I needed the medications, it felt as if someone were asking whether I deserved to survive.

When the substance you take, or the behavior you engage in, makes you feel worthy when you've felt worthless, safe when you've felt threatened, connected when you've felt alone, powerful when you've felt weak, or alive when you've felt dead inside: well, the natural reaction is to defend that substance or behavior with your life. Because to you, it *is* your life.

It took an explicit, honest, and compassionate statement—"It's not your fault"—for me to hear anything besides blame and accusation. How my doctor approached that conversation allowed me to hear the next part.

Whether an addiction started with a prescription or from drugs on the street, the missing ingredient for someone getting better is rarely to have another person give them a list of everything they've done wrong or what they should have done differently. The road of blame and accusation only leads to silence and shame. Recovery, and ultimately the responsibility that is needed, begins with healing.

Healing instead of blaming

Jesus' disciples see a blind man and ask him, "Rabbi, who sinned, this man or his parents, that he was born blind?" (John 9:2).

It is easy to hear the parallel to today. We hear another story of addiction and we wonder, "Who sinned, this person or their parents, that they are addicted?"

Cause and effect. Action and consequence. Fundamental to the natural sciences is the understanding that everything has a cause. We don't just accept that things are happening; we want to know *why* they are happening. And we want not just the physical explanation, what philosophers sometimes call the "material cause," but the meaning and purpose, or "ultimate cause."

The disciples' question reveals not just their desire to understand cause but their hope of assigning a moral significance to the cause. They want to know: Who is to blame?

For many, the logic of cause and effect was broken out into a simple system. Things that were deemed good had good causes, and things that were considered bad had bad causes. Blindness, being considered a bad thing, must have had a bad cause. This logic seemed so fundamental that the only debate the disciples could imagine was whether the blame should fall on the man himself or the parents.

Jesus interrupts this moral equation with his answer: "Neither this man nor his parents sinned; he was born blind so that God's works might be revealed in him" (John 9:3). Jesus proceeds to spit on the ground, make some mud, rub it in the man's eyes, and order him to go bathe in a nearby pool. When he does, the man can see.

Jesus exposes the folly of the desire to assign blame. Instead, he decides to heal the man in need. At the same time, he introduces another problematic idea. Instead of blaming any human, Jesus points the finger at God. The man was born blind "so that God's works might be revealed in him."

Taken on one level, this sounds like a case of an insecure deity, as if God feels the need to prove something and decides to make a child blind from birth in order to make a point. If this is the answer for all unexplained human suffering, though, it gets even worse. Are people across the world suffering because God wants to show off?

But this story is not an explanation for why bad things happen; rather, it shows us how we should respond when they do. Jesus' actions expose the faulty logic of blame. The story reveals that the nature of God is found in the act of healing, not punishment.

What about responsibility?

But if there is no blame, how can there be responsibility? The story of Jesus reveals the faulty thinking in blaming a person (or their parents) for being born blind. But how does that speak to addiction?

Philosopher Hannah Pickard writes about working in a clinical psychiatric setting with individuals suffering from personality disorders and addiction. As she observed the practices of the professionals around her, she noticed that they were accomplishing two things that at first seemed contradictory. First, they held their clients responsible for their actions. Second, they suspended judgment and refrained from blaming their clients. At the same time.

One of the common characteristics of those with personality disorders, and certainly of those with addictions, is the tendency toward self-harm. Addiction is characterized by ongoing use of a substance or continuance of a behavior despite all the negative consequences. Threatening someone who is engaged in self-harm with additional harm is not only often ineffective; it can be counterproductive.

When people are treated as either good or bad, clean or using, sober or not-sober, they are incentivized to hide any possible transgressions. They know that one slip could ruin everything. Rather than motivate positive behavior, this encourages deception and disconnection. Fear of blame and the feeling of shame push us into a state of bad faith and fuel denial.

Pickard advocates what she calls "responsibility without blame." In this framework, which focuses on restoration, responsibility still matters. But instead of starting from a standpoint of blame, the focus is on understanding the source of actions. This requires a compassionate curiosity about what it will take to restore what is wrong.[1]

When friends and family members and professionals interact with someone struggling with addiction, a focus on restoration doesn't mean ignoring an action's consequences. It's just that the goal of a restorative approach is healing, not consequences.

One of the foundational truths of the Christian tradition is that punishment is not the only way to be transformed. Punitive measures are not the only means to making things whole and right. It might be the second chance that makes the difference. If it isn't the second chance we've been given to change, it might be the third, fourth, or fifth—or as Jesus says, we keep going with forgiveness until we reach "seventy times seven" (Matthew 18:22 KJV). The primary moral logic of an eye for an eye can be interrupted with grace.

What Pickard and others have discovered is that grace is not simply a nice religious sentiment or Christian cliché. Grace is not just a gesture of benevolence; it is a practical approach for growth.

Hafiz, a fourteenth-century Sufi poet, wrote, "Blame / Keeps the sad game going. / It keeps stealing all your wealth."[2] A focus on blame is a downward spiral. Not only does it fail in its intention, but it drains you of the very resources you need to make a positive change.

Moving away from blame doesn't mean you don't search for causes and reasons. But it does mean you shift the framework from one of accusation to one of participation in healing and restoration.

The scapegoats ← *Stigma*

The primary public policy and cultural response to this nearly forty-year overdose crisis has been to blame those who are addicted or those who are supplying. Our world operates with the logic that if we punish those involved severely enough, then this whole crisis will go away while never asking why people are using and selling in the first place. This is called scapegoating: the ways in which we blame a person or group of people and then banish or do away with them in the hopes it solves a larger problem. It often focuses on the consequences of what has gone wrong, not the source of the problem. Scapegoating has not only failed to address the drug crisis; it has actively contributed to its breadth and severity.

A brief look at the origins of this idea sheds some light on how it occurs today. Once a year, on Yom Kippur, the Day of Atonement, the high priest was instructed to select two goats. One goat would be selected by lot to be sacrificed to YHWH as a sin offering. The other was for "Azazel," the wilderness (or in some traditions, the "demon of the wilderness"), and became known as the "scapegoat." This goat had a peculiar fate. The priest, according to Leviticus, was to "lay both his hands on the head of the live goat, and confess over it all the iniquities of the people of Israel, and all their transgressions, all their sins, putting them on the head of the goat, and sending it away into the wilderness" (Leviticus 16:21).

French historian and philosopher René Girard used scapegoat theory as a way of understanding the development of both society and religion. As soon as there is more than one person who desires the same thing—especially when the supply is limited—conflict, Girard claimed, is inevitable. When desire for the same thing grows within a community, so too will conflict. Inevitably, someone is blamed for that conflict and is either driven out of the community or killed. Whoever gets kicked out or killed is the scapegoat.

Getting rid of the scapegoat never gets rid of the problem, however, although it might relieve some tension. The scapegoat might have played a role in the conflict, but that person is never the ultimate cause of the conflict. A communal act of punishing, killing, or banishing the scapegoat will often provide a temporary modicum of peace. Everyone will see the consequences of the conflict in their community. Others will temporarily restrict or control their desires as a result of seeing the scapegoat punished.

This, Girard argues, is how human sacrifice is likely to have evolved. After a moment of conflict, a scapegoat is killed, and things seem, at least for a little while, to get better. The group or society then associates the violence with the resolution of the problem. Because they think it worked to solve their problem, they do it again the next time tension arises. Scapegoating soon moves from a one-time response to a particular situation to a ritualized act.

The Jewish people stood out in ancient history for not killing people to satisfy their gods. What Girard sees happening during Yom Kippur is a way of undermining the scapegoat process. The priest and the people know that the goat is not to blame for everyone's sins. The sending away of a literal goat shows the failed logic of blaming a person as a scapegoat. Simultaneously, it provides a ritualized moment in which all the people confess their sins and admit their wrongs. This is in stark contrast to gathering and punishing one person for the conflict in which everyone was involved.

In Girard's reading, Jesus takes on the role of the ultimate scapegoat. Jesus is an innocent who suffers execution under the hands of the Roman state, one of the bloodiest and most vicious empires ever known. Crucifixion was a regular form of execution at the time. The fact that crucifixion was a slow, painful, and public death was a means of control over the lands the Romans occupied.

The Romans did not believe that every person they sacrificed was the cause of their problems. But they realized the violent logic of scapegoating could be taken even further. With full knowledge, they would kill innocents. These mass murders would sometimes take place along the sides of the roads leading to major cities. The constant threat of violence, they knew, would help them maintain control over their subjects. *Pax Romana*, or "Roman peace," was built on the reality that the "few" would die to maintain order for the many.

It is hard to imagine the brutality of such an approach, and we'd like to think it was relegated to the ancient world. But it isn't that easy to get rid of scapegoating; it often just changes form. Theologian James Cone, in *The Cross and the Lynching Tree*, reminds us that the crosses of Rome are not far from the lynching trees of the American South.

Lynching was a form of public torture and murder by a dominant majority exercising control over a vulnerable minority. The victims were burdened with the conflict and corruption of the community itself. Cone writes, "Until we can see the cross and the lynching tree together, until we can identify Christ with a 'recrucified' black body hanging from a lynching tree, there can be no genuine understanding of Christian identity in America."[3] The lynching tree is a negation of the fundamental message of Jesus and the reality that the cross represents.

Jesus demonstrates the failures of scapegoating while also unveiling the *Pax Romana* as the corrupt, violent illusion that it was. When we participate in any system of scapegoating, it is a denial of everything Jesus did.

Scapegoating always requires another scapegoat. The society that practices it develops a tolerance. One scapegoat is not enough. More are needed. Then more. There will never be enough scapegoats. Azazel has an endless appetite for the violence and lives that it is fed. This food only strengthens the beast, and it will not stop until the society consumes itself. Scapegoating is an addiction, and we, as a society, are in deep denial.

When lynching culture finally began to recede, the bloodthirst sought out a new way to continue the tradition. While the days of humans sacrificed on alters by a priest are long gone, scapegoating is as strong as ever.

Contemporary human sacrifice lives on. It goes by the name of the War on Drugs.

6

Other

In the mid- to late nineteenth century, the primary demographic addicted to opioids were middle-class and wealthy white women. One U.S. doctor at the time, R. Batholow, noted he was particularly concerned about any "delicate female, having light blue eyes and flaxen hair."[1]

Opium was prescribed widely for "women's issues" and for women of "nervous" character. In some circles, opium use would have been less likely to be frowned upon than the use of tobacco or alcohol. The substance had little or no regulation at the time and was available over the counter and freely prescribed by doctors.

Regular users were known either as "opium eaters" or, in polite society, as people with an opium or morphine "habit." Excessive use might have carried some social stigma, but people who used opium were primarily a focus of pity or concern. "What we think about addiction very much depends on who is addicted," writes David Courtwright in *Dark Paradise: A History of Opium Addiction in America*.[2]

The Harrison Act of 1914 turned opium and cocaine from substances readily available at any local pharmacy into illegal contraband. But the first laws about opium products were actually passed in the 1870s. Interestingly, these laws targeted only opium *smoking*, the primary mode of opium use for

Chinese immigrants. The campaign against this culturally specific form of use took off after the end of the gold rush, when
white settlers were having to compete with the more recently
settled Chinese immigrants.

The Harrison Act was also passed at a time when both
cocaine and opium use were on the decline. The bill had
dubious chances of passing, especially with opposition from
Southern senators concerned that it would be a violation of
states' rights. Champions of the legislation circulated rumors
of Black "cocaine fiends" and spread unsubstantiated stories
of Black men, fueled by the drug, raping white women. The
resulting racist hysteria secured the remaining votes.

"Reefer madness" was initiated by Harry Anslinger, a
federal agent who had enforced alcohol prohibition but saw
his department shrink after the Eighteenth Amendment was
repealed in 1933. There was little reason to believe that marijuana use had grown, and there was no public demand for it
to be banned. Still, he campaigned to crack down on the drug
and expand his own budget. He told stories of violence and
murder, including one of a Florida youth who had smoked the
"killer weed" and then went on to murder his entire family
with an axe. But the group he claimed were made the most
violent of all? Mexicans.

Heroin users were soon referred to as "hopheads" and
"junkies." The moral model taught that those who sought
out and enjoyed the drug did so because they were morally
corrupt. Those who became addicted were weak-willed. Low-
lifes sought out those of otherwise good character, pushed
their drugs on the weakest of them, and pulled them into
their fold.

The primary people who were addicted were no longer delicate females with blue eyes and flaxen hair. They were mostly
poor men who lived in the city, and were racial and ethnic
minorities and recent immigrants.

Don't forget: what we think about addiction very much depends on who is addicted, and therefore whom we blame.

Psychologists say that most of us suffer from "asymmetrical agency bias," or that we make "fundamental attribution errors." These are serious-sounding ways of noting that when things go well for us, we tend to think the outcome occurred because of the things we did right. When things go wrong, we focus on factors outside our control as the primary causes. We don't believe that the rain falls on the just and the unjust (Matthew 5:45 KJV), but that the rain is our bad luck and what other people deserve.

My story of addiction is relatable to a lot of people—especially those who can imagine me as someone they know, love, and care about. Those who are middle-class, white, and college educated may feel that connection most of all, but if you are any of those things, you might feel a sense of affinity to my story. But the greater moral test is our capacity to relate to stories that are not like our own.

In fact, the "relatability" of my story could cut both ways. It can implicitly draw a line in our heads between the "sympathetic" and "vicious" addict. Maia Szalavitz, an author and journalist specializing in addiction, notes that sympathetic portrayals of those who suffer from addiction—portrayals that move readers and observers to act compassionately—may be rooted in altruistic motives. But, she writes, such characterizations can have unintended consequences: "highlighting 'innocent' white people whose opioid addiction seems to have begun in a doctor's office sets up a clear contrast with the 'guilt' of people whose addiction starts on the streets."[3]

If anyone reading this book walks away thinking there is a strict division between "deserving" and "undeserving" people when it comes to addiction, I have failed. For far too long, decision-makers and political leaders have drawn these lines not because of public safety or our common well-being but because it is easier (at least for a while) to find a scapegoat than it is to restore what has been broken.

Crack

The crack cocaine crisis of the 1980s and 1990s was our first opportunity to address some of the many causes of addiction and push back the tide of this long unfolding overdose crisis.

We failed. This failure has come at the cost of hundreds of thousands of lives, the devastation of Black and Brown communities and the tragic loss of human potential through mass incarceration.

Crack in America, one of the most comprehensive books published on the topic, locates the crack cocaine media frenzy from roughly 1986 until 1992. "Newspapers, magazines, and television networks regularly carried lurid stories about a new 'epidemic' or 'plague' of drug use, especially crack cocaine," write editors Craig Reinarman and Harry Levine. "This 'epidemic' was spreading rapidly from cities to the suburbs and was destroying American society. Politicians from both parties made increasingly strident calls for a 'War on Drugs.'"[4]

In January 1985, 23 percent of Americans identified nuclear war as the "most important problem facing this country today." Only 1 percent answered drugs. But in July 1986, the three major news networks dedicated a total of seventy-four evening segments to the subject of drugs, with half of those about people addicted to crack cocaine.[5] President Ronald Reagan recommitted the country to a War on Drugs, which President Richard Nixon had first announced, and politicians of both parties jumped on board.

Between October 1988 and October 1989, the *Washington Post* alone ran 1,565 stories about the drug crisis. In September 1989, President George H. W. Bush used his first prime-time national address to confront the drug that was "turning our cities into battle zones" and "murdering our children."

The devastation was real. Crime and murder rates surged in neighborhoods across the country. Cocaine-related emergency room visits more than doubled in a few years. The death toll from both overdoses and drug-related crime mounted. Soon after President Bush's 1989 national address, 64 percent of Americans believed that drugs were the most important problem facing the United States. Now only 1 percent answered nuclear war.

But that isn't the whole story of crack cocaine or the War on Drugs. Just as U.S. drug policy had focused on racialized targets for generations, the war was declared not so much on a substance as on a small group of users, the latest scapegoats.

The media coverage and legislative push about crack cocaine did not coincide with actual numbers of total drug use or even of cocaine use more broadly. Reinarman and Levine write, "The number of Americans who had used any illegal drug in the previous month began to decline in 1979. . . . Lifetime prevalence of cocaine use among young people (the percentage of those twelve through twenty-five years old who had 'ever' tried cocaine) peaked in 1982, *four years before the scare began*, and continued to decline after that."[6]

Cocaine use, across the entire population, had been on the rise in the 1970s, not the 1980s. By the time coverage of the "epidemic" started, fewer people were using cocaine regularly in any form than they had in years. What shifted was that among wealthy and middle-class white users, powder cocaine use decreased, while use of crack cocaine increased among lower-income Black users.

Remember: what we think about addiction very much depends on what we think about who is addicted, and changes who gets punished.

"Crack was a marketing innovation," the editors of *Crack in America* note.[7] What was once an expensive and thus "high-class" drug—cocaine—was repackaged into smaller and less expensive portions. The high, since it was smoked instead of snorted, hit faster and harder. For a cheaper price, you could forget about your circumstances, even if it wasn't for very long.

Smokable cocaine had been around before, but it was not widespread, because it lacked a wide market and distribution network. The mid-1980s provided a base of potential work-ers with few other economic prospects who were desperate enough to take the risk of dealing.

Crack cocaine didn't cause a wound on the American urban landscape. It was a deadly infection that spread in an already open wound. Michelle Alexander, in her book *The New Jim Crow*, argues that "the decline in legitimate employment opportunities among inner-city residents increased incentives to sell drugs—most notably crack cocaine." Crack cocaine offered a release as "the anger and frustration associated with joblessness boiled."[8]

Alexander does not diminish the damage and related violence the drug left in its wake. But the drug was not a sole cause. It was the combination of poverty, inequality, hopelessness, and discrimination that created the context for addiction to take hold. Wealthier users of powder cocaine had the resources to seek expensive treatment and stave off many of the negative consequences for longer than poor users could.

Alexander writes, "As a nation, though, we had a choice of how to respond."[9] Instead of treating the underlying causes, the response was almost entirely punitive. The budget for the Drug Enforcement Agency (DEA) ballooned from $2 billion in 1981 to $12 billion in 1993. Spending under the George H. W. Bush administration hit $45 billion, more than all other presidents since Nixon combined, and it was spent almost entirely on law enforcement. In 1986, Congress passed a law distinguishing powder cocaine from crack cocaine and dramatically increased sentences for the latter. But there is no pharmacological difference between the drugs, only a difference in delivery system and the skin color of their primary users.

By 1992, one in four young Black men were in jail, in prison, or out on probation or parole. The percentage of the U.S. population behind bars was unprecedented in human history. Bill Clinton solidified mass incarceration as a wholly bipartisan approach, overseeing the largest increase of federal and state prison inmates of any president in American history.[10]

The War on Drugs led to mass incarceration, our modern-day human sacrifice. The scapegoats were cast out. Politicians, and much of the public, believed that they had found the right people to blame: Black men and other men of color. They believed the primary challenge left was to "clean up the streets" and round up enough people in the hopes that Azazel would soon be satisfied.

Black, Brown, and normative whiteness

"Instead of getting rid of a drug, we tried to get rid of people."[11]

Ed Stetzer, now executive director of the Billy Graham Center, was a white pastor in a church in Buffalo, New York, in a community hit hard by the spread of crack cocaine in the late 1980s. When he saw people in his congregation, both Black and white, struggling with addiction, he says, "I could care for them as their pastor, but when it came to public policy, my response was 'lock them up.'"

Stetzer reflects on his response then and compares it to his reaction to the opioid crisis today. "In our rush to protect *our* communities, *our* families and *our* values, we sought to put distance between 'us' and 'them,'" he writes. "We made groups, constructed labels, and tried to do everything we could to separate what we perceived as the 'clean' from the 'unclean'—in many cases, the white from the black."[12]

Stetzer did not set out to be discriminatory. But he admits, in retrospect, that he saw the dealing and use of crack as "black

street crime" that deserved punishment, not treatment. Brian
Broome says the racialized dichotomy can be summed up this
way: "Black means addict, white means victim."[13]

When people like Stetzer become oriented toward empathy
and treatment for people struggling with addiction, it's a positive change. Recent public policy responses have stepped away
from some of the more punitive models of addressing drug use.
But in a series of papers, researchers Helena Hansen and Julie
Netherland track the racial differences in cultural perception
and public policy between the rise of crack cocaine and opioids. They warn about the "whitening" of the opioid epidemic.

Because most opioid overdoses occur among white users,
resources for treating drug addiction are being funneled primarily to white and relatively wealthy communities. But these
resources aren't going to other communities that also need
them. Because of the disparity, overdoses in Black communities
are now growing at a faster rate than in white communities.
We have the beginnings of a new two-tiered system, Hansen
and Netherland argue. The first continues to treat people of
color who are addicted as criminals: with punitive incarceration. The second system treats white people as victims of a
disease: with treatment.

An analysis of more than a hundred mainstream articles
on the opioid crisis found that white people were consistently
portrayed sympathetically, as users, while people of color were
pictured as criminals, in handcuffs.[14] Another study notes that
the moral model, and the punitive approach to drug policy
that came with it, was not questioned by politicians until the
rise of prescription opioid addiction in the 1990s and 2000s,
when white prescription opioid use, addiction, and overdose
deaths began to surge.

For more than a century, racist drug laws have hurt and
damaged all the communities they were intended to punish.
But scapegoating does not only ultimately fail; it makes things

worse. It creates an illusion of a solution while the real infection spreads. It creates a false sense of security because it perpetuates the belief that we have found the heart of the problem and dealt with it. The lines we draw in us-versus-them arguments not only hurt the "them"; they can destroy the "us."

"If we had invested in harm reduction programs and increased the availability and quality of addiction treatment" at the time of the crack epidemic, Hansen and Netherland write, "we would have been better positioned to reduce the toll of the current opioid crisis."[15]

A primary message of the War on Drugs was that poor people and Black people are more susceptible to addiction than the rest of the world. They became the scapegoats. Drug addiction was not seen as something fundamentally wrong with our society writ large; it was something wrong with "those people" and "those communities." If there was societal dysfunction, it was *theirs*. Punishing *them* through incarceration, and fighting the War on Drugs more generally, would solve drug overdoses and drug-related crime.

What this perpetuated was the idea that if you are a good working- or middle-class white person, then you are relatively safe from getting addicted. Those who became addicted were simply more prone to addiction, the thinking went. This took the form of anything from an assumption about an inherent moral superiority of white people to a belief in a kind of tragic genetic predisposition among people of color.

In 1999, the rate of drug overdoses showed some racial disparity. The overdose rate for Blacks was 7.5 per 100,000, for Hispanics, 5.4, and for whites it was 6.2. Then, between 1999 and 2016, the opioid overdose rate among whites increased 525 percent, among Blacks it grew 194 percent, and among Hispanics, it rose 74 percent. The rate in 2016 was 25.3 overdose deaths per 100,000 for whites, 17.1 for Blacks, and 9.5 for Hispanics.[16]

Hansen and Netherland argue that the assumption that white people are less susceptible than others to addiction earned white people the "privilege" of being targeted by drug manufacturers with opioid medications that the companies claimed had little risk of addiction.

This is how normative whiteness can hurt white people. Normative whiteness isn't an expression of European American culture but an erasure of those cultures into a dominating norm that isolates, dominates, and excludes. Ruby Sales, a civil rights activist and author, distinguishes between European Americans and a "culture of whiteness." Whiteness, she argued in a 2018 talk for the New Baptist Covenant Summit, "is no culture . . . it is simply skin." When we reduce people to their skin color and disconnect them from their history, it results in a kind of "soul suicide."

The culture of whiteness that Sales addresses is a myth of inherent superiority. White culture became an idea of social and cultural attainment divorced from a particular heritage, a form of dislocation and fragmentation. And dislocation, as we will see, is a fertile ground for addiction. Normative whiteness directly oppresses those that it excludes but is also an illusion that has inherent danger for those doing the excluding.

Political power and economic wealth can keep at bay, for a while, some of the consequences of dislocation. Dislocation negatively affects those who are already vulnerable in the first place. Instead of seeing already vulnerable populations as the canary in the coal mine, too many white people looked around and said, "I sure am glad I'm not a bird!"

Women
We need to challenge the myth of redemptive violence perpetuated in our desire to find a scapegoat. This goes beyond the harmful myths surrounding ideas of normative whiteness and also encompasses a distorted view of masculinity.

Author and philosopher bell hooks argues for the important distinction between masculinity and patriarchy. Masculinity can be a good and healthy expression of gender identity. Patriarchy is a distorted understanding of masculinity that relies on dominance and control. It holds up a false or narrow idea of masculinity and declares it the normative standard by which all things should be judged.

In creating a culture that is not so prone to addiction, philosopher Bruce Wilshire argues that we need to "stop habitually modeling ourselves on a male deity that stands above Nature and owns and controls her."[17] In an upcoming chapter, we will see the many ways that our desire to control can lead to an addiction, and ultimately to our loss of control. Wilshire argues that our obsession with control is fueled, at least in part, by an understanding of God as a completely transcendent judge who exercises divinity through total control.

A distorted view of God as the ultimate patriarch leads to a distorted view of masculinity and brings us to a desire to control things we can't or shouldn't try to control. As we'll explore later on, feelings of control were at the heart of my own addiction experience. It is little wonder, then, that at a time when white men have experienced themselves as having less control, they have reached for substances which they feel help them regain control.

In the late nineteenth century, when opioid addicts were mostly white women, we can see the way that distorted views of masculinity and femininity hurt women directly. Male doctors were highly likely to prescribe high amounts of opium to women for their "female complaints" and "nervous" natures. Under a purported rubric of care and concern for women's inability to deal with pain or the difficulties of life, women were given opium.

High opioid addiction rates among women weren't just a medical phenomenon; there were social aspects as well.

David Courtwright notes, "Opiates also suited the purposes of frustrated women whose aspirations had been blocked by a male-dominated society."[18] This was a time of change for gender roles in the world. A burgeoning middle and upper class meant a larger population of women who no longer spent their hours in the laborious economics of the home. At the same time, culture limited other means of self-exploration and meaning making. One woman of means wrote, "I am the last woman in the world to make excuses for my acts, but you don't know what morphine means to some of us, many of us, modern women without professions, without beliefs. Morphine makes life possible. It adds to truth a dream."[19]

Morphine, she admitted, had taken the form of a religion in her life. It allowed for her to imbue with meaning the many activities that would otherwise seem meaningless.

The belief in white male dominance as the rightly ordered structure of the world was and is a lie. The dissolution of that lie can be a painful one for those with something to lose. But the consequences of the lie, both for those who have benefited from it and for those who have suffered from it, are real. A false myth, increasingly difficult to believe, has led us to a place where hundreds of thousands are dying from deaths of despair.

7

Despair

Henry David Thoreau wrote in *Walden* that most people "lead lives of quiet desperation."

That desperation is no longer quiet. It is raging.

The opioid crisis cannot be reduced to the crisis of a chemical; it is a symptom of an epidemic of despair. Researchers Anne Case and Angus Deaton have noted a uniquely American trend: more middle-aged white people are dying.

After decades of declining mortality rates—primarily because of gains in treating cancer and heart disease—the likelihood of a white person dying between the ages of forty-five and fifty-four has gone up. A similar trend has not been seen in any other of the world's wealthiest nations.

If the mortality rate for this group had stayed at 1998 levels between 1999 and 2013, nearly 100,000 fewer people would have died. If the gains had kept pace with what they were between 1979 and 1998, then nearly 500,000 fewer people would have died.

The change was driven almost entirely by drug and alcohol poisonings, drug- and alcohol-related liver disease, and suicides.[1] These deaths have become known as "deaths of despair." When the false hope of scapegoating others inevitably failed, and economic opportunity slipped away for those who once had it, the crisis of confidence that President Carter described, and the malaise that came with it, spread.

People are dying because they feel that they don't have enough to live for.

Acedia

Early Christian monks had a name for this kind of despair: acedia. Acedia is typically translated as "sloth," but cultural connotations of laziness or idleness don't convey the original meaning. While some expressions of acedia may include an avoidance of productive work, acedia is an exhaustion with life and a profound loss of meaning. Philosopher Karl Clifton-Soderstrom gives a broad definition: a "depressed-like state that can afflict us during the middle of the day, the middle of the week, or the middle of life—where task becomes tedium, vocation becomes vacuous, ritual becomes rut, and where we can no longer experience the vitality of life or the goodness of love. Acedia afflicts one with the mundane wherein the everydayness of our lives bears down upon our once-impassioned souls as if to remind us, 'Vanity of vanities! All is vanity.'"[2]

Acedia can afflict those who are out of work and those who work one hundred hours a week. It is a state of uncertainty as to whether work or life has meaning and purpose at all.

Researchers Deaton and Case, in a follow-up report on mortality rates, tell a story of what they call "cumulative disadvantage."[3] The demographic driving the increase in mortality rates for white people is non-college-educated and working-class whites. There was a time when a young white man could reasonably expect to leave high school, take a job at the factory where his father worked, and do just as well or better economically than his father did. A college degree nearly guaranteed a good job upon graduation. This is no longer the case.

The researchers note that 90 percent of those born in 1940 were better off by the age of thirty than their parents were at that age. Of those born in 1960, only 60 percent were better off by 1990 than their parents were at age thirty. This downward trend has continued.

Wages declined, but this drop was masked for a while as an increasing number of women entering the workforce kept household incomes up. Slowly, various forms of economic and social support faded away. As Robert Putnam details so well in *Bowling Alone*, institutions and organizations that used to provide connection, a sense of purpose, and both formal and informal means of support began to decline. Membership in labor unions, church attendance, and participation in voluntary groups declined at the very same time that marriage rates were falling and divorce rates were climbing.

It isn't hard to imagine the former coal miner in West Virginia or factory worker in Ohio. They put in decades of demanding physical labor. They pushed through their pain because they found purpose in their work. Then, when they were laid off, they found themselves with nothing to think about but the pain in their backs or knees. It isn't long before a day can be filled with and then revolve around a substance that provides some distraction or relief.

Deaths of despair are not just about income. Wages for Black and Hispanic workers are consistently lower than those for whites. In fact, income-wise, Black workers with some college education have fared worse than their white counterparts.[4] But while Black and Hispanic mortality rates have been higher, across the board, than those of whites, they still improved over this period. The gap has been closing—not because we have figured out how to make things better for everyone, but because things have gotten worse for already poor white people.

"If you've always been privileged, equality begins to look like oppression," says historian Carol Anderson. Feelings of being oppressed, whether grounded in reality or not, can lead to hopelessness. For those in long-marginalized communities who had come to expect oppression, any sort of gains may be cause for hope. In fact, Anderson claims, it is that "sense of hopefulness, that sense of what America could be, that has been driving black folk for centuries."[5]

For generations of Black Americans, challenge, oppression, and segregation were the norm to be expected. For many white Americans, however, the system had worked relatively well. When the system failed white people, there was a profound experience of loss. For Black Americans, that failure was more of the same.

Opium of the masses

Rising drug overdoses, alcohol-related deaths, and suicides are not distinct phenomena. Each one represents a path of acedia. When hundreds of thousands of individuals decide to give up on life at the same time and in the same ways, we need to reflect on a broader societal failure to create a context of meaning and connection that makes life worth living. Systems that failed some for a long time are now failing a greater and greater number.

The simultaneous growth of drug overdoses and suicides blurs the lines between them. Many overdose deaths are the result not of a conscious choice to end one's life, but rather of a slow descent into a life that is no longer being lived. Existence has become anchored to the use of a substance—use that is frequently an attempt to make life manageable but ultimately cuts it short.

Karl Marx famously called religion the "opium of the masses." He argued that the working class was becoming aware of the absurdity of their own situation but that religion was getting in the way. Religion, in his reading, was a means of justification for and distraction from the oppression of the ruling class. It served as an anxiety-reducing delusion that distracted people from the meaninglessness of the work they had available to them.

Today, *opium* is the opium of the masses.

While deaths of despair have recently proliferated in the lives of working-class and poor white folks in America, it would be a mistake to believe that a college education or relative wealth is protection against acedia. Karl Clifton-Soderstrom quotes the fourth-century monk Evagrius in what sounds like a description of the lives and days of many white-collar workers today:

> First, [acedia] makes the sun appear sluggish and immobile, as if the day had fifty hours. Then he causes the monk continuously to look at the windows and forces him to step out of his cell and to gaze at the sun to see how far it still is from the ninth hour, and to look around, here and there, whether any of his brethren is near. Moreover, the demon sends him hatred against the place, against life itself, and against the work of his hands, and makes him think he has lost the love among his brethren and that there is none to comfort him. . . . He stirs the monk also to long for different places in which he can find easily what is necessary for his life and can carry on a much less toilsome and more expedient profession.[6]

Maybe you can imagine this in your own life. We no longer look at the sun but at our phones to see what kind of time has passed. We don't look *out* of our cell but *at* our cell, flipping to a social media stream and scrolling through what our friends are doing. While we scroll, we develop a resentment that our own lives are less fun and fulfilling than the lives of our friends.

The here and now, the people who are around and present, pale in front of the manicured and curated versions of another person's life. We begin to wonder, like Evagrius, if we have lost the love of our friends, and we begin to believe that there is "none to comfort" us.

So we fill our evenings with overeating, because it feels comforting, or binge-watching our favorite show, because we are so tired that we just need to "relax." We split our attention between the screen of the television and the screen of our phones. Indeed, one of the most effective ways to avoid the gnawing questions of meaning is by staying busy enough to avoid them. A constant flow of information and distraction turns the mind and the heart away from the abyss of asking *why*. Why do we worry about tomorrow? Why do we toil and reap? What is the treasure of great price that all our lives are working toward?

When we do pause between activities, we try to fill the void. We forget that we are more than our work or the things that we produce. Our busyness represents a profound loss of freedom, and one that occurs through a gradual winnowing away of what it means to be human. We replace what it means to be a person with a shallowness of activity.

Is Sisyphus happy?

Sisyphus is the mythic king known for the punishment he received from the gods: to push a stone to the top of a hill, only to have the stone roll back to the bottom. The task then was to start again, knowing that the stone would always roll back down, and do so for all eternity.

When French philosopher Albert Camus writes about Sisyphus, he makes a troubling comparison: "The workman of today works every day in his life at the same tasks, and this fate is no less absurd. But it is tragic only at the rare moments when it becomes conscious."[7] Biola University philosopher Kent Dunnington, in response to the idea that addiction seeks reward without work, writes that addiction may actually be rooted "in the suspicion that modern work is without rewards."[8]

This suspicion—the fear that all that society offers is a chance to forever push a stone up a hill—is not new. The difference today is how widespread the belief is. The previous mythology, what Ruby Sales calls "the culture of whiteness," is disintegrating. The rust of acedia is quickly eroding its foundations, which have proven to be far more brittle than previously assumed. But the illusion of what once was is hard to shake.

"One must imagine Sisyphus happy," concludes Camus. Why? Because Sisyphus knows that there is no end to his pushing a boulder up the hill. He is under no illusion that his task is anything more or anything less than it really is.

It is this fact—that he is fully conscious of what he is doing—that allows him to be happy. He commits himself to the work. "Each atom of that stone, each mineral flake of that night-filled mountain, in itself forms a world," writes Camus. "The struggle itself toward the heights is enough to fill a man's heart."[9]

Camus concludes that life is worth living, even if we don't know or can't understand its meaning. He recommends against taking the leap of positing a greater religious and spiritual meaning to our existence. That, he believes, is a kind of psychological crutch.

While I don't believe that Camus is ultimately right about the universe or the role religion can play in our lives, he points to something deeply true about the world we have created. When, as President Carter noted, human meaning is defined by what one owns, we have indeed created a context in which there is no ultimate meaning. "Piling up material goods cannot fill the emptiness of lives which have no confidence or purpose," Carter claimed,[10] and the attempt to do so is indeed an absurd Sisyphean task.

A materialist society, no matter the economic system at work, destroys meaning and purpose when it reduces people to the measure of their economic activity. When people have no other means by which to measure the significance of their lives, it is little wonder that so many choose to end it when they see the possibility of economic prosperity slip away.

At the heart of the despair that drives the addiction of so many are not detached questions about existence and meaning. Instead, this despair is often undergirded with a universal human experience that demands a response: pain.

8

Pain

To understand addiction we need to understand the pain the addiction addresses.

The pain that led to my addiction began late on a Wednesday night in November. I was twenty-five years old.

I had stayed at the office late and then come home, eaten dinner, and watched a show before bed. Then I felt it: a blade churned in my stomach. It pushed to get out. I grabbed my stomach and leaned forward, and then I leaned back, hoping that the blade would stop moving. But it dug deeper, twisted. I felt nauseated. I had eaten a salmon burger, so maybe it was a fishbone moving around in my stomach? Or bad fish? It still felt like a blade was twisting. It must just be some food that needs to keep moving, I thought. Maybe it was gas? I went to my bed and lay down.

I breathed deeply and tried to keep the nausea under control. With each expansion of my chest I felt new knives, smaller knives, poking out from my stomach to my ribs. I lay on my stomach, but the pressure pushed the knives around inside. I moved to my back and felt the weight of the room pressing down on my exposed stomach. I flipped to my side and tried to breathe short, shallow breaths. I fell asleep and then woke up to the sound of my own moaning. I tried to stop, but the moaning got louder. It was coming from deep inside where the knives were. It was coming from a place beyond me.

I made my way to the bathroom and tried to vomit. Whatever it was that had taken over my body, I needed to get it out. I sat on the toilet, but it only seemed to spread the pain. Morning, I kept thinking about morning. My face was hot. I let myself fall to the floor and lay on the cold tiles. For some, a night on the linoleum means moral reflection and heartfelt commitments to never drink tequila again. But this night I just prayed for the sun to rise.

I clenched every muscle in my body, trying to fight the pain, push back the knives. They cut back, cut deeper. By four in the morning, I couldn't wait any longer. The sun was still too far off. I called a cab.

An emergency department is not a democratic institution but a strictly controlled oligarchy. First impressions with the triage nurse can make or break your visit. If it doesn't look like death is imminent, you can wait. If your blood flow has soaked through the bandages but is no longer spurting, then you can take a seat next to the guy with the mystery cough and the woman with the goiter that keeps looking at you.

I struggled between telling the triage nurse just how bad the pain was and maintaining a New England granite–inspired stoicism. I also made a new deal with the pain. Now that I was talking to the nurse, I told my pain that it shouldn't suddenly go away. It had been consistent for the past six hours, and I had prayed for it to go away. But now that I was at the hospital, I wanted the knives to perform. To evoke the deep moans of someone who is suffering.

No performance was necessary.

I soon saw a doctor. No, I hadn't been doing any illegal drugs.

"On a scale of one to ten, how bad is your pain?"

"Eight."

"That bad?" the doctor asked. "With ten being the worst pain you've ever experienced."

I thought for a moment as the knives turned.

"Ten," I told the doctor.

"Addictions always originate in pain, whether felt openly or hidden in the unconscious," writes Gabor Maté, a Canadian author and addiction specialist.[1] The pain that night was from pancreatitis. The initial hospital stay started the path to the procedure that went wrong, which caused acute necrotizing pancreatitis, which meant months in the hospital and months at home and was when the addiction settled in.

My story is attached to medical terminology and diagnoses. I have reports detailing in precise medical language the origins of my pain. One of my early doctors suspected that the cause of the initial pancreatitis was a small gallstone lodged in my common bile duct. He was the one who initiated the exploratory procedure. I saw later, in his notes, that while the duodenoscope was able to access the pancreatic duct, it could not access the common bile duct. The doctor tried for an hour, and each time his scope went into the pancreatic duct. The repeated attempts enflamed the organ and resulted in necrotizing pancreatitis.

Human suffering has never been wholly captured by a doctor's notes. The medical reports and technical language do not make my addiction legitimate. Similarly, a story that begins with a party or on the street does not make an addiction illegitimate. If, as Maté argues, all addictions originate in pain, we might use different language, but each story shares a common thread.

Part of understanding addiction is understanding pain and our relationship to it.

The purpose of pain

Most of us have a deeply ambivalent relationship with pain. We want to avoid pain, but we don't want to be the kind of person who avoids pain. We don't want to be in pain, but we take great pride in letting others know that we can handle the pain that does come our way. Almost everyone rates themselves well above average when it comes to their pain tolerance.

Acute pain has a purpose. It is the alarm system of the body to alert the brain that something isn't right. The pain experienced when you place your hand on a hot stove is the reason you jerk your hand away. The intensity of that experience creates such a strong memory that most young children need only experience one burn to learn the lifelong lesson of being careful around a stove.

The experience of pain releases hormones like cortisol and adrenaline. I was once in a car accident and walked around dazed for twenty minutes, insisting that I wasn't injured—until a paramedic noticed a dark stain growing on my pant leg. He sat me down, cut open my pants, and revealed a gash that cut straight to the bone and required multiple levels of sutures to close.

Our brain's capacity to momentarily shut down or blunt pain is a valuable adaptive trait that allows for escape from danger. While it's rare, some people are born with a congenital insensitivity to pain, a disorder that disrupts a normal ability to experience pain. People with this disorder are often subject to severe injury as infants and children and have a higher likelihood of premature death. A life without pain is not a blessing but a curse. Pain is a sign of danger or threat. Not knowing there is a threat is one of the greatest forms of danger.

While studied as a medical phenomenon, pain also carries a sense of moral meaning. The Latin root for the word *pain* is *poena*, meaning "penalty" or "punishment." In Middle English, the word *pain* did not refer to physical pain in general but specifically to suffering caused by punishment.

The book of Job, thought to be the oldest writing in the Hebrew Scriptures, is dedicated to pain. Why do people suffer?

More specifically, are there connections between one's moral status and the existence and extent of one's pain? The book of Job doesn't provide easy answers. What it does provide is a clear condemnation of easy and simplistic ones.

Millennia later, we still ask questions about pain. Our questions haven't gone away. When we experience pain, or when we witness the pain of others, we tell stories that try to explain it.

Stories of pain

Addiction is rooted in attempts to relieve some kind of pain. Yet it is also defined by a persistence in pursuing the object of addiction *despite* the pain that pursuit causes. And once the addiction settles in, it is fueled by an avoidance of the pain that comes with withdrawal.

In this sense, addiction is a contradiction. It is the simultaneous pursuit of something that causes pain and avoidance of pain. But it is a contradiction many of us live with every day. Let's examine the two pursuits—the seeking after pain and the avoidance of it—a bit more closely.

On the one extreme is a kind of glorification of pain. "No pain, no gain" and "Pain is just weakness leaving the body" are common sayings in the world of exercise and sports. In this rubric, perseverance in pain is a sign of great strength. The capacity to suffer becomes the dividing line between the human and the superhuman.

This sort of narrative can take on a religious bent and connect to ideas of self-mortification and the cross as primarily a representation of suffering. The logic of this narrative is that Jesus admonished his followers to take up their cross; the cross means suffering, and therefore suffering is the calling of a well-lived life. Given stories of monks whipping themselves or kneeling on cold hard stone for hours at a time, the "mortification of the flesh" has long been a part of the Christian tradition. Proverbs 20:30 says, "Blows that wound cleanse away evil; beatings make clean the innermost parts."

At its best, this understanding of pain as cleansing and purifying can provide encouragement in the hardest of times. It can serve as inspiration to sacrifice one's own comfort on behalf of others in need. At its worst, it promotes an obsession with suffering that fails to acknowledge a goodness of the world and the beauty that can exist in all our lives.

This kind of pain ethic has been mythologized in my own family. Growing up, we all heard the story of our grandmother getting seven stitches in her forehead without any kind of pain medicine or anesthesia. So when I had a chainsaw accident one day and came into the farmhouse with a gash in my leg, I wasn't expecting too much sympathy. My grandmother quickly found alcohol and bandages for the wound. As I was getting patched up, she also found some duct tape, explaining that it was to put my pants back together so I could go finish my chores. We were going out to eat that night to celebrate my brother and sister-in-law's anniversary; the restaurant was right near an urgent care center, she informed me, so I could go there after dinner.

Later that night, when I finally got to urgent care, the doctor asked, while stitching up the wound, why in the world I had waited so long. I responded, "You don't know my grandma."

At the other end of the spectrum is the avoidance of pain and the impulse to fight against it. This pain ethic manifests itself in helicopter parents who look to protect their children from every scrape and bruise or possible discomfort. It shows up in patients assuming that every ache and pain must be medicated and avoided at all costs.

But it also shows up in the belief that blessings come to those who have faith. Those who don't have such "blessings" or who are struggling must be at fault for the state of their affairs. Poverty or disease are counted as outer manifestations of an inner state.

A fight against pain can be motivated by the best of intentions. Scripture is full of passages about fighting against injustice and oppression. The presence of poverty and suffering isn't necessarily the result of an inner state of those who are hurting; instead, poverty and suffering exist because of dysfunction within society.

There is the very basic desire to give good things to the people you care about. "Is there anyone among you who, if your child asks for bread, will give a stone? Or if the child asks for a fish, will give a snake? If you then, who are evil, know how to give good gifts to your children, how much more will your Father in heaven give good things to those who ask him!" (Matthew 7:9-11).

So I use the word *ambivalent* to describe our understanding of pain, because most of us do not simply choose one of these narratives of pain. Most of us hold both at the same time and in sometimes conflicting ways. The narratives we use to describe our own pain, as well as the pain of others, are often a Rorschach test for our beliefs about the world.

Destroyer of words

The nature of pain is such that we can never fully know the pain of another.

With pain, especially chronic pain, we fear that we will not be believed. That fear creates a defensiveness that creates a distance from those who might be able to help. "To have great pain is to have certainty; to hear that another person has pain is to have doubt," writes professor Elaine Scarry.[2]

Anyone who suffers from chronic pain, especially in a way that is not immediately evident to the outside world, knows what it feels like to not be believed. Those who are in pain can't help but know their own pain. They might wish it otherwise or try to escape it, but this is beyond their capacity. Their efforts to distract themselves and focus on something beyond this world of pain are often futile or work for short moments at best.

When you observe someone else's pain, you might experience doubt, especially when that pain is invisible to you. Cuts, bruises, swollen ankles, severely broken bones: while these are visible to others, much pain is not so observable. We read facial cues, body language, and attempts at verbal articulation, but none of these things allow us to directly translate that person's internal experience into something we can measure.

To be believed about your pain, you need to be able to describe it. You need words. But words are often among the first things that pain steals.

Pain resists verbalization, argues Scarry. Our initial reactions to pain are the nonverbal and guttural: cries, screams, shrieks, writhing, cringing, and wincing. The loss of ability to say much at all says the most about the intensity of the pain.

Love, awe, or wonder can make us feel that we don't have words to express the depth of what we feel. Still, people manage to write sonnets, poems, plays, and songs that try to capture the ineffable. For these and similar emotions, we keep giving more and more words as we try to find the words to express what we feel. But pain resists those sorts of descriptions. The most powerful depictions of pain are often not words at all but our preverbal grunts, cries, and screams.

This inability to verbalize and bring others into our world is a force that separates us from others, especially when the pain is not easily visible. Without words for the level of pain I was experiencing, I began to rely on the next best thing: medical tests and scans that would prove to others and justify to myself the intensity of what I was experiencing. A bad test result wasn't bad news, but an affirmation of an inner state that I couldn't communicate any other way.

In the months after my hospitalization, I spent hours writing about the pain I had experienced, grappling with how to express it. One of my recurring descriptions was of "the knives." To me the knives were almost sentient beings, which had been angered and were set on taking over my body. Outside interlopers, they had made their home in my body and were wreaking havoc. As the pain grew, however, my experience of it changed. I no longer experienced pain as a foreign, outside force invading my body but as the betrayal of my inmost being. My flesh had turned on me and sought revenge for unnamed wrongs.

After that, the distinction faded. I no longer experienced myself as a person with a body that was in pain. I had become pain itself. I had ceased to exist, and only the pain was left. The pain had become more real to me than I was to myself.

No matter how much I wrote, my words never seemed to adequately express the experience of that sort of prolonged pain. In some moments of writing, even months after the pain had departed, I could feel my heart race and my body brace, as if awakening the memories of those days might just be powerful enough to bring their return.

One of the most important things my doctor said to me was, "I need you to know that I will never take away your pain medicine when you need it." His words dropped my defenses. I knew I was believed. He understood what I was going through and the important role the pain medicine played in my life.

When he asked me to take less pain medicine when I could, and when he invited me to begin exploring alternative ways of dealing with my pain, I was able to hear him. I never would have responded to his request that I start taking less pain medicine unless I first believed that he believed me.

Would you trust someone who tried to take away the thing that had given you comfort without addressing the source of your pain? Offering both an alternative and the support to explore it does not guarantee that a person will find recovery. But there isn't a great chance of progress without these gifts.

Long-term pain is not just an event; it can shape our experiences of the world. Joint pain can eat away at the edges of our world by limiting our ability to accomplish basic household tasks. Back pain can end a career. Pain can become the backdrop against which everything in our life is set. It can become the horizon toward which everything in our life moves. Pain can destroy the world we once knew and become the world we now know.

Making a strict delineation between "legitimate" and "illegitimate" addictions is to repeat the same mistake the disciples made by asking "Who sinned?" of the man born blind. If we want to move past the blame and scapegoating, we need to ask what is ours to do to help heal the pain that started the addiction in the first place.

While I opened this chapter with the time and day my pain began, that was only the pain of the pancreatitis. We all carry pain and wounds simply because we are alive. As I'll explore later, the opioids first addressed the pain that brought me to the hospital, but they also began to provide a response to other sources of pain—pain and need about which I was not yet even fully aware.

9

Sin

Being an eleven-year-old boy in a Christian home can be a bit miserable. I believed in a God who was a slimmer version of Santa, sitting up in the sky taking notes on whether I was bad or good and probably knowing everything I was thinking. My voice cracked, testosterone flowed, and I was petrified by the idea that anyone might be aware of my innermost thoughts.

I walked around with the near terminal guilt of knowing that I had committed adultery in my heart every day at least three times before breakfast. The theological concept of total depravity sounded like either a poorly named cologne or an accurate description of exactly what was going on in my early pubescent brain.

These early years of adolescence were marked by a deep fear that I was uniquely and exceptionally sinful. At any moment, the entire charade of my eleven-year-old innocence might come crashing down. While original sin was supposed to be a universal condition, I experienced it as something that somehow was especially true of me. It sounded as bad as the photos of diseased genitalia we were shown in our sex ed class. I believed that if anyone actually knew the thoughts that went through my head, they would know that I wasn't just your ordinary, run-of-the-mill sinner, but the kind who needed a special extra-strength grade of salvation.

I have to admit up front that I don't love the word *sin*. *Sin* has often been synonymous with "things I don't like," and *sinner* with "the people who aren't like me." In dominant Christian culture, the idea of sin has been used as a battering ram of shame. And the concept has done a great deal of harm when used to describe the actions of particular people who struggle with specific addictions and as a convenient way to ignore the actions of others.

Yet we cannot do away with the theological category of sin. Sin is the expression of evil in the world. Sin clings to individuals and groups and societies. The overdose crisis and now the opioid epidemic are clear expressions that sin is real.

We need an understanding of sin that goes beyond the individual and to the communal. While a consequence of sin can be separation from each other, our concept of sin can be one that binds us together in a common struggle.

While it would be easy to think about sin as primarily applying to those struggling with addiction, I don't think that is the case. The evil that is at work in the overdose crisis and the opioid epidemic are expressions of what theologian Walter Wink has called "fallen Powers." "Evil is not just personal but structural and spiritual," Wink writes. "It is not simply the result of human actions, but the consequence of huge systems over which no individual has full control."[1]

Evil was operative in criminally negligent pharmaceutical companies and market forces that pushed for fast and cheap answers to pain. It was present in the unethical physicians who fueled the early rise of opioids, and it was lodged in the actions of a family pharmaceutical dynasty whose name now adorns a wing of the Metropolitan Museum of Art in New York City.

Let me explain.

The Powers

The year of my hospitalization, my bottles of pills and patches of fentanyl represented a handful of the 243,738,090 opioid prescriptions that were written. That is 79.5 prescriptions per 100 people in the United States. That was 2009, and prescription rates would keep climbing for another three years until they peaked in 2012, at 81.3 written for every 100 people.

Reporter Sam Quinones writes in *Dreamland* that beginning in the 1970s, the global medical community began paying increased attention to the role of pain in a patient's recovery prospects. Beginning with dying cancer patients and those with other painful terminal conditions, doctors rethought the role of narcotics, after decades of relatively little outpatient use.

The World Health Organization (WHO) developed a ladder for pain treatment steps and described morphine as an essential drug in that mix. The WHO also declared that freedom from pain was a universal human right. Quinones summarizes the sentiment and its effect: "If a patient said he was in pain, doctors should believe him and prescribe accordingly. . . . Worldwide morphine consumption began to climb, rising thirtyfold between 1980 and 2011."[2]

The 1980s and 1990s saw the rise of the palliative care movement, which transformed pain medicine access for those who were dying. Pain soon became known as the "fifth vital sign," and doctors were encouraged to monitor and treat it. With increased interest in treating pain came increased investment from pharmaceutical companies in long-lasting opiates.

Quinones describes a split that took place in the medical community. On one side was a holistic movement of pain care, exemplified by the Center for Pain Relief at the University of Washington Medical School, which integrated a variety of disciplines to help treat and manage long-term pain. Social, psychological, and other medical factors were all taken into account. Patients might work with a physical therapist or social worker in addition to receiving prescriptions, when appropriate, for opioid-based painkillers.

But another movement was gaining steam as well. This side argued that doctors should let go of their fears of patient addiction, which had long restricted morphine prescriptions. Much of this perspective was based on what was sometimes referred to as a "landmark" or "extensive" study published in the *New England Journal of Medicine*, which claimed that fewer than 1 percent of those treated with opioid pain relievers ever became addicted.

But there was no such study. There was only this: a small letter to the editor, which looked at a limited data set of patients given opiates under highly controlled hospital settings after surgery. The authors of the letter had stumbled upon what they thought was an interesting data point. The writers of the letter did not speak at all to outpatient prescribing or long-term treatment of pain with opioids. Then, in what became a dangerous game of telephone medical research, the letter was cited repeatedly in other journals, lectures, and research.

In 1996, the FDA approved Purdue Pharma's OxyContin as a "minimally addictive" pain medicine. All Purdue's salespeople were trained to quote the nonexistent study as gospel truth. They encouraged doctors to increase their prescription levels. Insurance companies were hesitant to reimburse more comprehensive pain treatment when a pill would do just fine. The company funded lavish meals, trips, and gifts for their top-prescribing doctors, and it pursued new doctors who would champion their products. Doctors could earn hefty fees by participating in speakers' bureaus, lecturing on the drug and encouraging their colleagues to explore its many uses.

Unethical doctors and criminally negligent pharmaceutical companies continued to pump out pills across the country. Williamson, West Virginia, is a town of 2,900 with two pharmacies just four blocks apart. Over a ten-year period, 20.8

million opioid painkillers were shipped there, roughly seven thousand for every man, woman, and child.[3] But instead of analyzing such information and sounding the alarm, drug companies used high prescription rates as a way to discern where the most profitable areas of the country were and then sent more salespeople there. Federal prosecutors found that company executives were well aware of widespread abuse of their product but nevertheless continued their aggressive campaign to downplay risks of addiction.

Purdue Pharma's person-to-person contact with doctors was working. Their branded pads of paper, mugs, and pens were everywhere. Sales reps were compensated well, making up to $100,000 a quarter in bonuses alone.[4] Many doctors were ready to believe what they were being told, and many patients came to expect pain relief when they wanted it. There were few reasons at this point for doctors not to go with the flow.

Some doctors, like David Procter, knew exactly what they were doing. Procter eventually served eleven years in prison (the sentence was shortened after he testified against former colleagues). He is known as "the godfather of the pill mill." Procter's clinics, with doctors who would see over 150 patients a day for as little as three minutes each, would have long lines stretching outside. His clinics' doctors would write prescriptions for up to two million pills a year.

In 2007, Purdue Pharma executives pled guilty for their "misbranding" and deception in the marketing of OxyContin. The company was fined $634 million, a small fraction of the more than $35 billion in revenue the drug produced for the company. Litigation against the company continues across the country, as the death toll rises and societal costs mount.

The overdose crisis in the United States was already well underway by the time Purdue Pharma's OxyContin came along. But the aggressive marketing, blatant deception, and concerted choice to ignore the warning signs helped create the opioid epidemic we see today. It is a perfect depiction of "the Powers" as Wink defines them: systems beyond any one individual's control, systems in which evil circulates and perpetuates itself. The evil and destruction is reflected in but is still far beyond the choices of any individual.

Which brings us back to the family whose name adorns the north wing at the Met, a wing at the Louvre, and a museum at Harvard: the Sacklers. Purdue Pharma was founded by Arthur Sackler, known for revolutionizing pharmaceutical marketing and creating one of the largest family fortunes in American history. They built that fortune, in part, on these deadly, unethical, and illegal practices.

At the same time, one could say that the Sacklers and their company were also trying to solve a very real problem. A study from the Institute of Medicine estimates that nearly 100 million Americans suffer from some sort of chronic pain. That translates into 25.3 million reporting that they have experienced pain every day for the previous three months, at a cost to the nation of $635 billion in treatment and lost productivity.[5]

The Institute of Medicine notes that the average medical school education devotes just nine hours to the study of pain, and estimates that there are only four thousand physicians in the country who are certified, currently practicing pain specialists.[6]

There is a huge need to address pain. When the government began cracking down on opioid prescriptions, some legitimate chronic pain patients lost access to drugs they need to function. There are now blogs and websites dedicated to cataloging the suicides of those who lost their treatment and felt they could no longer handle the pain.

"The Powers don't simply do evil," writes Wink. "They also do good. Often they do both good and evil at the same time. They form a complex web that we can neither ignore nor escape."[7] Purdue Pharma and other pharmaceutical companies have gotten off too easy. But painting the company as the personification of pure evil fails to acknowledge the complexity of the crisis. Evil and sin often work in much more insidious ways. We can acknowledge some good intentions while simultaneously exposing the evil that has been done.

Evil tends to cascade downward, expanding in force and power. Yes, there are those who are addicted who might steal, deceive, hurt, or even kill others in the midst of their addiction. But their limited power reduces the range of their damage.

Jesus was known in his ministry for welcoming those who were on the outskirts of society and typically known as "sinners." He saved his harshest critique for the evil done by those in power.

For those at the top of multibillion-dollar corporations, sin lives in ignoring reports of abuse, skirting guidelines to make it to market before a competitor, pressuring subordinates to do whatever it takes to reach sales targets. The people making these compromises may be gainfully employed and respected in their communities. Their names may grace the halls of museums and art galleries.

The most dangerous and deadly drug dealers in the world tend to wear expensive suits.

In this together

Philosopher Friedrich Nietzsche, in *On the Genealogy of Morals*, argues that Judeo-Christian morality is based in resentment and is a system built with the aim of getting and keeping power. By punishing certain sins, religious leaders believe they can maintain the status quo and consolidate power.

Nietzsche was right about morality, at least some of the time. Leaders of all stripes have indeed used the language of morality to justify their power grabs. In Christianity, it isn't unusual to pick out specific "sins" as a way to consolidate the flock, as opposed to emanating from a genuine desire for moral growth. Preachers can be intent on convincing their congregations that the world was created in six literal days about six thousand years ago—and claim that Jesus was just being hyperbolic when he told his followers to sell all they had and give their money to the poor. Churches can reject a loving and committed same-sex couple on the basis of some verses in Leviticus—while claiming that verses about welcoming foreigners and immigrants are relics of a bygone age.

With the crack epidemic, public policy responded to the actions of individuals, not the evil that the Powers are capable of. Millions of scapegoats were sacrificed in our criminal justice system, and evil only grew.

This understanding of a structural and systemic evil does not preclude personal sin. We can stop "the sad game" of blame that Hafiz identified and still talk about responsibility, but in a different way. Catholic mystic Thomas Merton provides a helpful perspective in *New Seeds of Contemplation*: "To say I was born in sin is to say I came into the world with a false self. I was born in a mask. I came into existence under a sign of contradiction, being someone that I was never intended to be and therefore a denial of what I am supposed to be. And thus I came into existence and nonexistence at the same time because from the very start I was something that I was not."[8]

Merton's take on the concept of original sin is that we are all born into a state in which we are struggling to realize our truest identity. When we say that we are sinners, we refer to a state of being we share with everyone around us. Our own actions can contribute to this mistaken identity, but so can the culture we swim in and the institutions that surround us.

In this way of thinking, the "sin" of the opioid crisis is not primarily any individual's choice to use or not use drugs. It is a reflection of something deeper. Chronic pain patients can feel like themselves again for the first time in years when properly prescribed pain medication. And those same people, though taking the same drug, can lose themselves if they are gripped by an addiction that grows beyond their control. Sin is evident in the striving for lost identity.

Contemplative James Finley reflects further on the thinking of Thomas Merton: "Sin is not essentially an action but an identity. Sin is a fundamental stance of wanting to be what we are not. Sin is thus an orientation to falsity, a basic lie concerning our own deepest reality. Likewise, inversely, to turn away from sin is, above all, to turn away from a tragic case of mistaken identity concerning our own selves."[9]

Adam and Eve hide from God after eating the fruit, illustrating the separation. But hiding is never just hiding from another; it is always also hiding from oneself. To be separated from God is to be separated from one's truest self.

The idea of original sin isn't supposed to make this problem of addiction worse by making everyone feel bad all the time or feeling a constant sense of foreboding shame the way I did in early adolescence. The idea that, as Paul puts it, "all have sinned and fall short of the glory of God" (Romans 3:23) is actually the antidote. It is the connection someone feels when they come to an AA meeting for the first time and hear everyone in the room confess that they struggle in the same way.

Original sin, when understood well, lets us know that we are all in this together. That the struggles we face, which make us feel alienated from others, mean that we can actually be open and honest with those around us. If others are honest, they will admit they are struggling. Far from increasing any guilt and shame we feel, this concept of original sin can help us heal and grow.

We inherited this struggle with sin. Ancient theologians used to argue about how exactly sin was inherited. There was, for some thinkers, a biological component to it. If we understand "original sin" as an inborn disconnect between our will to do what is right and our capacity to execute it, then they are exactly right.

We have a hard time doing the things we want to do and *not* doing the things we don't want to do. Sin is actually built into the person you are, all the stuff you inherited. The idea of original sin is an ancient acknowledgment that we will be in conflict with ourselves. Still, this inherited sin never destroys, but only covers up the original blessing bestowed when God declared all of creation not just good, but very good.

One of the great contradictions inherent in my story is that when my doctor told me I was addicted to my pain medicine, he also reminded me how much I had needed it. I had been in acute respiratory distress; my pancreas was destroying itself; and other organ functions were in decline. Pain, under these circumstances, wasn't just a discomfort to be endured but a threat to my life. The high levels of stress hormones could have contributed to potentially fatal complications.

Opioids have taken the lives of so many, and they could have taken mine. Yet for a time, opioids not only made a painful condition endurable but very well may have saved my life.

10

Substance

Opioids are simultaneously medicines and poisons. They save lives and they take lives. They relieve pain and they can cause pain. They are not the cause of addiction even though they are addictive.

For most of human history, the resin from the poppy flower was seen as both a gift and a blessing. Its botanical name, *Papaver somniferum*, means simply "sleep inducing." Today, it is hard not to imagine a kind of sinister intent residing behind the white, pink, or classic crimson petals. The sleep is not one of rest but final repose. Joy and sleep, bravery and forgetting, alleviation of suffering and the coming of death: all were seen in the poppy flower.

Stone Age evidence of opium poppies in the area that is now Switzerland predates the fermentation of alcohol.[1] The Sumerians, ancient pioneers of agriculture, began cultivating the poppy plant in lower Mesopotamia between the Tigris and Euphrates Rivers nearly five thousand years ago. As the developers of the written language, the Sumerians also give us the first recorded name for the flower. They called it the "joy plant."[2]

The poppy's medicinal and beneficial uses were discovered early on. In the oldest medical document ever discovered, the Ebers papyrus, opium is included in seven hundred remedies.[3]

Galen, the Greek physician, claimed it was a wonder drug and "resisted poison and venomous bites and cured, amongst other things, headaches, vertigo, deafness, epilepsy, apoplexy, poor sight, bronchitis, asthma, coughs, the spitting of blood, colic, jaundice, hardness of the spleen, kidney stones, urinary complaints, fever, dropsy, leprosy, menstrual problems, melancholy and all other pestilences."[4]

The poppy was so common in the Roman Empire that its symbol sometimes appeared on their currency. While it was known to alleviate pain and to allow users to forget their sorrow, it was also closely associated with sleep and death. Their god of sleep, Somnus (the brother of death), is depicted holding poppies. It was the drug with which Hannibal decided to take his own life.[5]

In Scripture, Jacob—or Israel, as he was then known—told his sons to bring gifts to Egypt during a famine in the hopes to trade for food. While many translations note that "spices," "balm," or "healing resin" were included in the gift, the Complete Jewish Bible is more specific; it says opium was included (Genesis 43:11). The Egyptians and others in the ancient world were apparently already well stocked: thebaine, an opium derivative, takes its name from Thebes.[6] Another city, Sicyon, became known as Mekone, or "the town of poppies."[7] The flower pops back up in Jewish history when it appears on bronze currency with the prince and high priest of the Maccabees, in the second century BCE.

The use of opium as a medicine continued for centuries. In the Middle Ages and up until the early twentieth century, opium products were the primary approach to treating dysentery because of the drug's constipating side effects. Its relaxing—and sometimes deadly—power over the respiratory system made it a common treatment for tuberculosis.

Oliver Wendell Holmes is quoted as saying, "I firmly believe that if the whole materia medica, *as now used*, could be sunk to the bottom of the sea, it would be all the better for mankind, and all the worse for the fishes." The one medicine he gave a pass to was opium, "which the Creator himself seems to prescribe."[8]

Opium products were so ubiquitous in the United States that morphine was more prevalent and easier to obtain in 1870 than tobacco was in 1970.[9] What were known as "patent medicines," many of which contained some form of opium or cocaine, boomed. Opium was prescribed, according to one historian, for "practically everything."[10]

The tree

Genesis teaches that there were two trees in the center of the garden of Eden; the tree of life and the tree of the knowledge of good and evil. Learning the story as a child, I thought of the tree of knowledge as bad, the source of all human suffering. Without the tree, we never would have gotten kicked out of the garden. I imagined that I certainly would never step away from paradise simply for a taste of fruit.

My confusion got deeper as I grew older. I knew my parents were smart enough not to leave something fragile in the middle of our living room. So why would God leave a tree capable of messing up the world for all people for all time just lying around like that?

But the tree was not the source of evil any more than it was the source of good. It represents the human capacity to know the difference between the two. The story is not so much about an ancient choice that was made as about an image of the choices we face every day.

This was not the story of a thoughtless deity setting up humans for a task they were bound to fail. The fruit was not a "demon" that carried inside it something evil. The morality of the situation was determined not by the nature of the fruit but by the actions of the eater.

In the book of Acts, Peter has a vision in which he is shown animals that are traditionally considered unclean. He hears the voice of God telling him: "Get up, Peter; kill and eat." Peter protests, but the voice responds, "What God has made clean, you must not call profane" (Acts 10:13, 15).

Jesus deals with a similar issue in an account in Mark 7. We read the story of Jesus' followers getting in trouble with local religious authorities for failing to adhere to traditional handwashing rituals before eating. Jesus' response? "There is nothing outside a person that by going in can defile, but the things that come out are what defile" (Mark 7:15).

Beyond specifics about food, Jesus also deals with religious traditions when he and his followers once again get in trouble for their failure to observe laws regarding the Sabbath. Jesus responds, "The sabbath was made for humankind, and not humankind for the sabbath" (Mark 2:27). The laws about the Sabbath, Jesus argues, are meant to serve, not be a burden. They have an intention behind them, and that intention is human flourishing.

The story of Adam and Eve eating the fruit can seem petty and vindictive if it is a tale of an insecure deity who doesn't want humans eating his favorite fruit. But it isn't. This story demonstrates that the will of God, the good of the garden, and the good of humanity are all the same thing.

Our search for the knowledge of good and evil is not an attempt to discern arbitrary laws created by a deity who wasn't smart enough to hide the source of temptation. Rather, our search for the knowledge of good and evil is the quest for how the world can work well and the dangers that surround us. Our own flourishing and that of all existence are bound up together.

The world is not a place filled with inherently evil things. The world is, as is repeated seven times in the first chapter of Genesis, made up of things God considers *good*. The knowledge of good and evil is an understanding of this truth: we can choose to be a part of the flourishing, or we can choose to be part of the diminishment of ourselves, others, and the world around us.

These designations—*good* and *evil*—are never arbitrary edicts from a vengeful deity. They are descriptions of what true flourishing—and true harm—can look like.

Demon drug

It would be easy to reimagine the story of Adam and Eve with a poppy flower at the center of the garden of Eden. Instead of the fruit of the knowledge of good and evil, it would be a taste of the resin of the flower of joy and suffering. If only Adam and Eve had resisted temptation and left the flower alone, we would still be in paradise today.

Imbuing a substance with a moral power is not uncommon. In the world of drug policy, it is called the "demonization of drugs." To demonize is to do more than point out the dangers of a substance; to demonize drugs means to ascribe a malicious power and intent to the drugs themselves.

Craig Reinarman and Harry Levine, editors of *Crack in America*, write, "This demonization invests the substances themselves with more power than they actually have. . . . Drugs, unlike viruses, are not active agents; they are inert substances. They do not jump out of their containers and into people's bodies."[11]

There are two great dangers. The first is to believe that any substance or drug is a "demon" with malicious intent. The second is to believe that it is entirely safe. Administered by a doctor through a slow-releasing transdermal patch, fentanyl provided relief for me. But a few too many grains of fentanyl can kill you. Even water, essential for our survival, is deadly at high doses.

Most people who are prescribed opioids don't develop an addiction or even problematic usage.[12] If you are an adult without a previous history of substance abuse and you take pain medicine as prescribed and are aware of warning signs, your likelihood of developing an addiction is relatively low. But here is the tension. As soon as you believe the pain medicine is "safe," you are opening yourself up to a whole lot of trouble. The crime of a company like Purdue Pharma was not in creating an inherently "evil" pill; the crime was lying about the potential dangers and creating a false sense of security against addiction.

Alcohol was once the demon drug in America. Leaders of the temperance movement believed that alcohol was not just a factor in addiction but the complete cause of it. Christopher Cook writes in *Alcohol, Addiction and Christian Ethics*, "Because drunkenness was essentially conceived as being a disease of the will, caused by alcohol itself, temperance in the traditional sense of moderation resulting from the use of reason was viewed as an oxymoron insofar as alcohol was concerned."[13]

This was why the temperance movement pushed for a complete prohibition. Prohibitionists did not believe there was such a thing as responsible consumption of alcohol, because the "demon" of addiction was caused by the "demon" in alcohol itself. They believed alcohol was the cause of bad behavior and direct moral degradation.

Billy Sunday, the prohibitionist preacher, predicted the day before Prohibition went into effect, "The reign of tears is over. The slums will soon be a memory. We will turn our prisons into factories and our jails into storehouses and corncribs. . . . Hell will be forever rent."[14]

Sunday's prediction failed to materialize. Criminalizing alcohol created a lot of criminals, but it didn't address the other factors that contribute to alcohol addiction. Individuals and groups aren't the only scapegoats. Substances can become scapegoats as well.

Still, I cringe when I hear anyone say a substance is "as safe as alcohol." Alcohol is not safe. It can be incredibly dangerous. Alcohol-related deaths still outpace drug overdoses in the United States, claiming the lives of over 88,000 people per year.[15] But as we will explore in subsequent chapters, the presence of a chemical in your body does not automatically create addiction. Addiction requires a whole host of factors. If we reduce our understanding of addiction to just the substance, we won't address the other causes. As with all scapegoating, the belief that you have eliminated the problem while other underlying causes remain creates a whole new risk.

Molecules of emotion

Jesus insists that God's laws are not things created before humans and therefore we are commanded to follow them. Instead, the laws exist to the extent that they serve human flourishing. When their purposes become perverted, Jesus breaks those laws and leads his followers in doing the same (see Mark 2:27).

When Jesus is asked why he is hanging out with the sinners—the rule breakers—he responds, "Those who are well have no need of a physician, but those who are sick; I have come to call not the righteous but sinners" (Mark 2:17). Morality is about health and well-being, not about conforming to arbitrary decrees.

All that is created is good. The law, or any kind of moral understanding, is meant to serve humans, not us to serve it. The will of God and human flourishing are the same thing.

We must hold in tension these facts: opioids can be a medicine and a blessing in one form and context, and they can be deadly poisons in another form and context. The difference is not in the substance itself but in our relationship to the substance and the purpose of its use. And if we dismiss the substance as entirely evil, we won't understand what draws people to these substances in the first place.

Opioid addiction is a particularly powerful kind not because opioids are foreign to our brains but because we have a long developed and important system designed to receive our bodies' natural equivalent: endorphins. In the 1970s, researcher Eric Simon named certain molecules he discovered in the brain *endorphins* as a mix between the words *endogenous* and *morphine*. They are endogenous because they originate inside us, and he used the word *morphine* because of the striking chemical similarity between the newly discovered molecule and morphine.

Endorphins are a powerful chemical and one we have in common with many other creatures on the planet, all the way down to single-celled organisms. Endorphins can ease pain, both physical and emotional, and are key in many functions we never even think about: from our heart rate to our breathing and the working of our intestines.

One of the most well-known functions of these endorphins is to bond mother and child. They help bond sexual partners and produce the euphoria experienced by bungee jumpers, skydivers, and extreme sports enthusiasts everywhere. "That was such a rush!" is the exclamation of a person in the throes of this powerful chemical. Endorphins have been called the "molecules of emotion."[16]

This chemical doesn't work on its own. To ensure that we don't develop a tolerance to our own supply of endorphins, the brain employs another chemical, called oxytocin, to increase the uptake of endorphins. Oxytocin increases the effects of endorphins so they last longer and are experienced more deeply.

This chemical cocktail is present and important since our infancy. If an infant feels stress, the caretaker can directly soothe them by addressing a need, such as changing a diaper or feeding the child. Over time, as a healthy bond is formed, the release of endorphins and oxytocin is triggered not just by the caring action, but by the presence of the caretaker. An infant will often begin to feel the soothing effect of those chemicals the moment a parent steps into the room.

The amazing capacity of the human brain to ease our pain, find comfort in distress, regulate our body's systems, bond with other people, and find pleasure in the daily experiences of our lives—this is the same capacity that allows us to become addicted to narcotics.

The systems of our brain that respond to opioids are not tangential to who we are. They are a part of our daily lives and flourishing. When they go astray, we go astray. Gabor Maté says it this way: "Addiction to opiates like morphine and heroin arises in a brain system that governs the most powerful emotional dynamic in human existence: the attachment instinct. Love."[17]

Addiction always mimics something we need. Opioids can provide a temporary boost for a natural system that can ease our pain. At their worst, they take over that system, narrowing our field of vision and disrupting our capacity to feel that love we so desire. This is when it feels like our bodies that were once our friends become our enemies.

11

Body

I didn't fully understand what it means to have a body until I was twenty-five and went into the hospital with pancreatitis. Just weeks before I had been going running almost every day. Now it was a struggle to breathe.

The first time I wet the bed, I cried. A nurse came and inserted a catheter. I didn't understand all the things going on around me, but I resolved to regain control. I could force myself back, I thought; if I could just focus, maybe then I wouldn't lose everything.

It wasn't long until I lost control of my bowels. I wept. Quietly. I stared out the window as I was cleaned for the first time since I was a child. A nurse returned with a diaper and wrapped it around me. I tried to protest but when I went to speak, no words came out.

I felt that same loss of control again months later in my struggle with the pain medicine. The pill would dissolve in my stomach, spread through my body, and the molecules would cross the blood-brain barrier and light up my opioid receptors. In those moments I would feel confident and in control. I would feel certain in my resolution that I would soon be done with these pills altogether.

A few hours later I would wonder if that was *really* the last pill I would ever have. The anxiety would spread from my head to the rest of my body. It wasn't just a thought or feeling but a demand from every cell of my being. Soon the control I had imagined vanished. I could no longer distinguish myself from the demands of every atom that constituted my body. My body became the only self that I knew. That self was in charge.

I lost control. Misfiring chemicals and misbehaving organs. The body I inhabit failing to respond to the will of my consciousness.

Being a body

Our bodies disappear from our awareness when they are at their best. We notice no difference between them and our will. We feel like the master of a machine that does our bidding where our own wish is our command.

It doesn't take much to disrupt this illusion. We miss a meal, and suddenly our friend who can't decide on a restaurant seems like an enemy engaged in a conspiracy to deny us sustenance. We miss our cup of coffee, and a loved one's morning greeting suddenly becomes an unwanted intrusion.

What I discovered in the hospital when I was twenty-five was not that I "have" a body but, rather, that I am embodied. Addiction reveals to us the very physical nature of our own reality.

We are not disinterested beings who happen to ride around the earth in a hunk of flesh that we control but that doesn't affect us. Who we are, and the decisions we make, are always and fully integrated into our bodies. Even the language of "having" a body is deceiving. We are embodied: we are made up of our physical parts but never entirely defined by those parts.

"Addiction is never purely 'psychological'; all addictions have a biological dimension," writes addiction specialist Gabor Maté.[1] At first, I thought of pancreatitis and my ensuing addiction as two completely different experiences; pancreatitis as biological, and addiction as psychological. But pancreatitis affected my psychological state and addiction disrupted my biology. Different organs were the source of each problem, but the distinction between "mental" and "physical" quickly blurred.

Just as I lost some control of my body during my hospital stay because of an injury to my pancreas, I lost a level of control over my body because of a change in brain function caused by addiction. Addiction slowly destroys the very parts of our brains that could most help us overcome our addictions.

Gray matter refers to the part of our brain that contains most of our brain cells. The white matter is the part that contains most of the connections between those cells. The gray matter is often associated with our senses, emotions, speech, decision-making, and self-control. The white matter relays messages between different parts of the brain and is also associated with both learning and action.

In drug and alcohol addiction, both white matter and gray matter are diminished. Maté points out that a reduction in brain size correlates with the years of substance abuse: "the longer the person has been addicted, the greater the loss of volume."[2]

The brain is just one organ of the body. Its role is distinct but not wholly separate from the rest of our selves.

Two brains

"The mind is a wonderful servant but a terrible master," an old Asiatic proverb says.

The experience of losing control can be as simple as the nights that we lie awake with worry. Over and over we keep thinking about our finances, or a relationship gone wrong, or the things we should have said in that conversation. We want to quiet our brain and move on to whatever is next, but the loops just keep playing, and it feels as if there is nothing we can do to stop them.

The feeling of wrestling for control of our thoughts is a common conundrum in philosophical, religious, and spiritual traditions. We are "double in ourselves," wrote the French philosopher Michel de Montaigne, known for his depth of insight into everyday experience. "What we believe we do not believe, and cannot disengage ourselves from what we condemn."[3]

Passion and reason for the Greeks; the spirit and the flesh in the Bible; the conscious and the subconscious for Freud; the shadow self and the self for Jung; system 1 and system 2 thinking for contemporary psychologist Daniel Kahneman; first-order and second-order desires for philosopher Harry Frankfurt: all these are examples of ways that people throughout history have described the different forces inside us that produce our actions and desires.

William Irvine, in his book *On Desire: Why We Want What We Want*, writes, "Our brains have not one center of control, not one part that wills, but multiple decision-making centers that independently come to decisions about what we should be doing with ourselves. They are like army generals who each has his own idea about what the battle plan should be."[4]

We do not have a centralized decision-making center of the brain, so it isn't surprising that we often feel double-minded. Most of us probably feel even more divided than that! Author and psychotherapist Richard O'Connor describes this as "two brains, not working together."[5] There are a lot more areas of the brain than two, but it is a helpful, easy rubric to grasp a couple of important ways the brain functions.

O'Connor describes the "automatic self" and the "conscious self." The automatic self handles much of our behavior most of the time. It is in charge of our heartbeat, breathing, digestion, and sending us signals when we are hungry, tired, or in pain. It's handling a lot all at once.

The conscious self is the part in which we are aware of our own thoughts and choices. It is what allows us to have conversations with others and set long-term goals. It also doesn't tend to be very good at doing more than one thing at a time.

For a long time, one of the primary ways of understanding the split was that "reason" and "spirit" were good, while the "passions" and "flesh" were bad. But there's nothing inherently bad or good about either the automatic self or the conscious self. Each has its area of expertise and functions best when it is deployed in accordance with its strengths. The problem comes when they are in conflict or are not communicating.

In fact, it is a breakdown in communication between the automatic self and the conscious self that is at the core of addiction. Systems developed a long time ago for good, adaptive reasons can be destructive today if they take over. Things we do automatically, or things we have learned to do nearly automatically, can get us into trouble in complex circumstances that require more reflective thought.

For example, more automated behaviors, like foraging, used to be what kept us fed. Slowly, through practices like animal husbandry and agriculture, our strategies for gathering resources have been taken over by our conscious brain. Both the automatic self and the conscious self still want to keep us fed, and this can create a tug-of-war about who is in control.

Strong signals of dopamine, along with cues for high-energy foods, certainly helped our species stay alive as hunter-gatherers. When high-energy food wasn't plentiful, dopamine signals kept the goal of attaining food right in front of us and motivated us to get the calories we needed.

Now, though, when high-energy food (albeit low nutrition) is relatively cheap and plentiful, the automatic self and conscious self can come into conflict. Our conscious self knows that we want to eat a healthy diet and maintain a reasonable weight. But breaking the automatic self of its drive to consume high levels of calories when they are available can be difficult.

The conscious self is relatively open to new information and to change in comparison to the automatic self. Thus, deciding that you are ready to change your diet and exercise more often is easy; actually doing those things is hard. The conscious self can "decide"—but if the automatic self isn't on board, then all bets are off.

The divide between these different selves exists naturally within our brains. The challenge is creating cooperation between these systems. To feel a split, to feel the push and pull, to be uncertain about direction: this is not an aberrant situation. The increased capacity for conscious thought is both a blessing and a burden as it comes into tension or conflict with the older systems of the automatic self.

Changes in the brain

The technology to watch our brains at work in real time has transformed our understanding of addiction. We don't just know that the brain changes; we can see how it changes.

Alcohol, opioids, caffeine, and other addictive substances, when present in the body, all affect the functioning of the brain. When you drink, you get drunk. When the alcohol wears off, you sober up. But repeated use creates long-term changes in the brain that don't immediately reverse, and these changes remain even after the substance is gone from the system.

A common saying in neuroscientific research is "What fires together, wires together." Our brains are full of complex connections and neural pathways. The creation of new pathways and connections allows us to learn and build memories. The more often the areas of the brain "fire together," the stronger grow the connections between them.

I think of my childhood memories of sledding down the big hill across the street from our house. The first few runs through the thick snow would be slow. But over time, the more runs we'd take, the more the snow would pack down and create a path, speeding up our journey down the hill. As kids, we knew that if we wanted to create an especially fast run, we needed to be consistent and stay on the same sledding path each time.

The same is true with our brains. The more we repeat a certain neural pathway, the stronger and faster it becomes. This is where dopamine comes in.

The dopamine system's primary function is learning. Addiction researcher Neil Levy writes, "Dopamine release is a signal that the world contains more rewards than was predicted. Natural rewards (say, food) result in the release of dopamine. Once an organism has learned that a cue predicts a natural reward, the cue (and not the reward itself) results in the release of dopamine: it is the cue that is unexpected, since the reward itself is expected, given the cue."[6]

In other words, dopamine is the signal our brain gives to say, "Hey! Remember what is happening right now. This could be important." And the dopamine system is also the one you might remember from Pavlov's famous experiment with his dogs. When he rang the bell and then fed the dogs, their salivation soon began not with the presentation of food but with the ringing of the bell. Maia Szalavitz makes the connection between the learning systems of the brain and addiction in her book *Unbroken Brain*, and argues that our primary model for understanding addiction should be as a learning disorder.

The presence of food as a reward can trigger the dopamine system, but so can behaviors. Imagine a five-year-old with a bat in their hands, swinging away at a ball on top of the tee. The first few swings are wildly amiss. Then they connect with the ball and it flies out in front of them. In that moment they experience a rush of excitement. Dopamine has kicked in. The world just provided a greater reward than the child predicted.

Soon the child is back, swinging away and missing the ball—until that magic moment of bat and ball connecting happens again. This continues as the child learns to better associate the correct movements and mechanics with the swing required to hit the ball off the tee.

Now the child can coordinate their actions to consistently produce the desired result. Once their desired result—hitting the ball—is no longer difficult or unexpected, the excitement fades. Dopamine is no longer released in the same way it was with those early hits.

The child realizes that the older kids aren't hitting the ball off a tee anymore; they hit from an adult's pitch. The spike of dopamine for the child now comes from the newly developed, and harder to achieve, skill of hitting a live pitch.

That child might not play baseball for the rest of their life. Years later, though, they pick up a golf club and hit a smaller ball off a tiny tee. The challenge is greater but the dopamine rush of a child hitting from a tee is similar to that adult hitting a straight drive seventy-five yards down the fairway. Like that child, they soon obsess about doing it over and over again.

This dopamine rush drives us to learn and explore. One reason evolutionary biologists believe that humans take so much pleasure in flowers is that we have inherited a dopamine reaction to them. Our ancestors learned that a flower was a precursor to fruit and that fruit was food. Flowers became a cue for the future reward of food.

What happens when an addictive substance enters the picture?

"Drugs of addiction all hijack the dopamine system, in one way or another," writes Levy. "Unlike natural rewards (that is, the rewards to which the dopamine system is designed, by evolution, to be sensitive to), these drugs cause the release (or increase the availability) of dopamine directly."[7]

A big rush of dopamine is interpreted by your brain, "Do whatever you just did again because that was way better than expected!" But now, instead of being motivated to keep learning a new skill or exploring our environment, we just keep doing whatever gave us that dopamine rush. While our alcohol consumption, drug use, or gambling might be destroying our lives, the sought-after dopamine spike will keep communicating to our brain that the world is better than expected.

With repeated exposure to any substance, our brains work to restore balance. If you ingest caffeine, your body tries to adjust to the continued intake, and works to restore a balance. As your body adapts, that means you need more of the same substance to get the same effect that you used to get.

Now that you have developed tolerance through your body's efforts to restore balance, another effect kicks in. When you try to *stop* using the substance, your body is thrown off balance, because it just made all those accommodations to take in more of it. When the substance is suddenly absent, alarm bells go off and you feel the stress and discomfort of withdrawal.

This means that your behavior is reinforced both positively (the presence of dopamine and other typically positive chemicals) and negatively (from the pain or discomfort you experience if you stop using).

Addiction is not, at its root, about liking the thing to which you are addicted—although you might like it at first. Addiction is about wanting it.

Dopamine is often linked with pleasure in our brains, but it is better understood as connected to desire. Dopamine continues to fuel and motivate our actions long after they are no longer pleasurable. In some circumstances, this drive pushes us to overcome adversity in the pursuit of an important achievement. Dopamine can drive us to do better and be better. But other times, as is the case with severe addiction, it can push people to pursue a course of action that destroys their lives long after they have stopped feeling any kind of pleasure at all.

In my case, the pain medicine had begun doing more harm than good. The medication now caused pain, both through shutting down my digestive system and by causing increased sensitivity to pain. But it didn't matter. For months, what had fired together, wired together. My brain had learned the lesson, over and over again, that taking the pain medicine relieved pain and brought comfort. The dopamine signal had been consistent and strong. The path in the snow had become well worn, and sliding down it was easy.

Genetics

Another common topic in the ways that our bodies can seem to fight against us involves our genetics. While there is no "addiction gene," there are genes that have been associated with higher rates of addiction to various substances. Many researchers believe that roughly half of a person's susceptibility to addiction could have genetic links.[8]

Accepting that genes may influence addictive tendencies may help us be empathetic toward those who struggle with addiction. Our genes are not our fault. Some people feel terrible the first time they take a painkiller; it isn't anything I did wrong that made me feel good the first time I did.

However, discussions of genetic predisposition in an individual have sometimes been extended to support accusations of "genetic inferiority" applied to an entire people group. This kind of thinking has been used as an excuse for the perpetuation of social and economic disparities. Why try to help a community if they are just going to squander the assistance on drugs or alcohol?

To address this issue, take a look at the exciting field of research in addiction studies called epigenetics. Epigenetic research focuses not just on what genes we carry but on why certain genes are active and why others aren't. In the debate of nature versus nurture, genes have been understood as a part of the nature camp, and our environment as a part of the nurture camp. Epigenetics, however, shows that interplay between the two is more complicated than you might think.

Certain genes are turned on or off according to chemical cues that are triggered by our environment. Gabor Maté and others believe that this is a key to understanding addiction. Current research suggests that high levels of stress hormones are a signal to our DNA that we are in a hostile and uncertain environment. The genes that get turned on and off are supposed to help us adapt to that environment.

Studies from the children and grandchildren of Holocaust survivors have shown that these changes can be inherited from generation to generation. In other cases, genes can be turned on or off over the course of a person's lifetime.

For a person born into a stressful environment, those signals might have turned on genes focused on survival behaviors. Someone born into a secure environment might have more genes turned on that help with long-term planning and impulse control. Change the environment for either person, and you could change which genes are expressed and which ones aren't.

Dopamine is released when there is something about your environment that is better than expected. When your body is prepared for a harsh environment, then the dopamine spike from food, drugs, or alcohol will be even more significant. That means a faster learning cycle and a stronger message from your brain: "That was good! Do it again."

Our bodies are constantly at work in ways we do not fully realize or understand. Just as there isn't a "demon" of addiction inside any substance, there isn't a "demon" of addiction inside our bodies or brains. Addiction comes out of essential systems and processes that get derailed. As epigenetics illustrates, addiction is also never just about what is going on inside our brains. We always need to consider our environment.

12

Home

In 1971, the United States was embroiled in the Vietnam War. While the extent and toll of the conflict was slowly becoming clearer, a battle inside America's own ranks was raging.

Vietnam is next door to the Golden Triangle, where the borders of Thailand, Laos, and Myanmar meet and where, at the time, most of the world's heroin was produced. For a long time, the primary product was a rough and rudimentary form of the drug with a relatively low potency. But in 1971, a new highly potent formulation of the drug, known as No. 4, became available to American GIs.

"Tens of thousands of soldiers are going back as walking time bombs," a military officer told the *New York Times*.[1] Overdoses were on the rise, and military leadership saw their efforts having little effect as soldiers switched from "grass" (marijuana) to "scag" (heroin). Grass was easily detected either by drug-sniffing dogs or when it was smoked during use. Dogs weren't trained to find the scag, and it could be snorted without any smell or smoked with very little.

The problem was pervasive. A 1974 study published in the *American Journal of Public Health* found that 43 percent of returning soldiers reported having used narcotics (mostly heroin) while in Vietnam.[2] Of that group, nearly half reported that their use had led to a full-blown addiction. This indicated that nearly 20 percent of soldiers in Vietnam were regularly using and addicted to heroin at the time of their service.

Heroin, for the servicemen, was not particularly expensive. But for the people who were producing, distributing, and selling it, it represented an incredible economic opportunity. The drug was available nearly anywhere and whenever it was desired.

While U.S. soldiers were exposed to the extreme stress and trauma of combat and the constant fear of ambush or attack, they also experienced long periods of boredom and mundane stretches in relative safety where they had ready access to the drug. Heroin was used to relieve the stress of battle and to fight back the hopelessness and worry of the times in between.

The U.S. government prepared for a surge of addicted service members, who they anticipated would return with both their addictions and their supply. But that 1974 study found something that the researchers had never seen before. Ten months after returning home, nearly all the soldiers they interviewed and on whom they conducted urine analysis simply returned to whatever their previous drug use was (or wasn't) before they left for Vietnam.

Some 20 percent of servicemen reported being addicted in Vietnam, but only 1 percent were addicted upon their return to the United States. The study authors wrote, "There have been no studies of addict populations in this country that show anything like the 95 percent remission rate after ten months, which is what a drop from 20 percent addicted while in Vietnam to 1 percent after Vietnam suggests."

Treatment for addiction while soldiers were in Vietnam was almost entirely useless. The rate of success was nearly inverted from what it was when the soldiers returned home. If we only understand addiction as what happens to a brain isolated from an environment, this doesn't make any sense. To figure out what happened, we need to look at addiction from an angle for which the disease model does not account.

Rat Park

Researchers like Neil Levy don't question the disease model because they deny that addiction creates changes in the brain. The impairment is real, observable, and increasingly quantifiable. Addiction, Levy argues, is indeed a disorder connected to the brain. The distinction he makes is that it always affects a person who is "embedded in a social context."[3]

The concern is that if addiction is understood primarily as a disease that is internal to the person suffering from it, then we will neglect the external factors that cause or contribute to addiction. If human bodies are treated like machines, then all that is necessary to "cure" addiction is the right kind of tinkering by a good mechanic.

Bruce Alexander, an addiction researcher in Vancouver, Canada, has long studied the effects of social context on addiction. He argues that we are mistaken when we assume that addiction is fundamentally an individual problem. That someone either has the disease or does not. That recovery only means that individual getting better.

That doesn't help us understand the phenomenon of the high rate of soldiers voluntarily abandoning their heroin addictions without treatment upon returning to the United States. But a "dislocation theory of addiction" might give us some insight. Alexander writes, "From this perspective, addiction is not so much a problem of aberrant individuals as a latent human potential that expresses itself universally under particular social circumstances."[4]

Alexander doesn't deny that a wide range of other factors including genetics, life experience, and individual choices play a role, but he believes they need to be put into the background because of the power of the social forces at play.

In 1978, Alexander and his colleagues set out to determine to what extent environmental factors played a role in
addiction. At the time, drug research was often carried out on
rats that were observed in Skinner boxes, a type of laboratory
chamber. An isolated rat in a small cage would be given access
to food, water, and some sort of mechanism for accessing a
drug. It was not uncommon to see a rat forgo food or pure
water in exchange for continually self-administering a drug
until death.

This led to the understanding of addiction as a condition
or a disease caused by changes in the brain that were, in turn,
caused by the use of the substance itself. But these researchers
noted that the environment in which these studies were conducted was always the same, and never the kinds of environments in which rats would naturally live. What if the addiction
was occurring not just because of the substance but because
the Skinner box would be a pretty terrible place to live?

The scientists created an environment that eventually
became known as "Rat Park." This environment had a community of sixteen to twenty rats of both sexes, more than two
hundred times the space of a typical research environment,
and plenty of scraps and tins for the rats to play with. At the
end of a tunnel, the rats could access water dispensers—one
that was pure water and another laced with morphine.

The rats in the new, more social environment showed little
appetite for the morphine. The researchers added sugar to the
morphine-laced water, but still the rats did not consume it at
the level of the rats in traditional cages. The researchers even
forced the rats to consume morphine for a time to ensure the
rats would go through withdrawal if they did not keep self-administering the morphine. But, Alexander reports, "nothing
that we tried instilled a strong appetite for morphine or produced anything that looked to us like addiction in the rats that
were housed in our approximation of a normal environment."[5]

For both the rats stuck in Skinner boxes and the men fighting in Vietnam, the environment mattered—both in causing addiction and, eventually, in overcoming it. Rat Park for the rats and homes for the men did not serve as fortresses of insurmountable protection against addiction, but they did provide contexts in which healing could take place.

Indigenous populations

North American Indigenous populations have long been plagued by high rates of addiction, particularly heavy drinking. And tragically, rates of suicide are also high, especially among younger people. Native peoples did not do this to themselves. Governmental policy in the United States and Canada created near perfect conditions for addiction to thrive.

For generations, the "Kill the Indian, save the man" mantra made it clear that white settlers believed that there was something inherently wrong with Indigenous people and their cultures. Forced enculturation and separating families became governmental policy. Parents had to send children to boarding schools, where kids received beatings if they were caught speaking their native language.

This cultural imperialism has long been coupled with violent prejudice, which continues to this day. A 2016 report from the Department of Justice showed that 56 percent of Native American and Native Alaskan women report having been raped or sexually assaulted. The vast majority of these assaults are committed by persons outside the victim's tribe.[6]

In that dangerous view of "genetic inferiority," there was a widespread belief that alcoholism in Indigenous communities could be explained by a simple genetic propensity. But Bruce Alexander notes in his research that if the key factor were genetics, you could assume that the devastation would occur within the first generation of the introduction of alcohol. This is not the case. He argues that while some Indigenous individuals in Canada did quickly take to excessive drinking when Europeans first introduced alcohol, "most individuals and tribes abstained, drank only moderately, or drank only as part of tribal rituals as long as they maintained an intact tribal culture. It was only during periods of cultural disintegration that alcoholism emerged as a universal, crippling problem for native people."[7]

Alexander tells the story of the Hudson's Bay Company, which was chartered in 1670 for hunting and trapping in Canada. Company records show that they specifically recruited employees from the Orkney tribe because they were known for being less likely to have drinking problems than their European counterparts. By 1779, 78 percent of the company's Canadian employees were Orkney. And things went well— until the men were brought to remote outposts with little contact with the outside world or their own traditions. It was then that alcoholism became a near universal problem in the tribe.[8]

These patterns, Alexander contends, hold true for other populations popularly known as heavy drinkers, like some of my ancestors, the Scotch-Irish. First, whiskey was introduced. While a few individuals might have drank heavily, the population as a whole maintained a moderate consumption level, mimicking the broader population. Then, with the rise of industrialization, many were pushed from their traditional agrarian-based lifestyle into rural poverty or crowded industrial tenements. It was *after* these cultural and economic changes that heavy drinking across the population skyrocketed.

One study, which took a wide-angle look at addiction rates among dislocated populations across the globe, found "a history of massive displacement and sociocultural disintegration that historically preceded problematic substance use at a population level."[9] In other words, some genetic propensity toward addiction did not cause the problems. Addiction was an adaptive response to major social dislocation. It was how some people were trying to cope with a stressful and dangerous environment.

The researchers noted three common and exacerbating factors. The first is stress. Moving to a new city or country under the best of circumstances can be a stressful experience. Forced or unwanted relocation is even harder. Add to that a minority status, socioeconomic disadvantage, and a distrust of institutions that have lied and broken promises to you and your family for generations, and it becomes surprising that even more Indigenous people haven't developed an addiction while trying to cope.

The most oft-cited reason for having a drink or using a substance of choice is to "relax." If you have limited options for lowering or dealing with your stress, habitual substance use becomes a pretty attractive option.

The second factor is changing norms and cultural identity. Dramatic shifts in location and movement away from previous norms—as with soldiers when they go into combat—can create a context for substance use that wouldn't otherwise exist. Young men who wouldn't consider using heroin back in their hometown might have fewer defenses while dealing with the stress of combat in a foreign country.

The same is true with a change in group identity. Substance use might be the center of or a marker for membership in a new group. College students who live on campus are more likely than their peers who commute to engage in heavy drinking, as campus social groups form and then begin to center on alcohol or drug use.

The third factor is trauma. Experiences of traumatic stress have been clearly linked with increased addictive behaviors. The landmark ACE (Adverse Childhood Experiences) Study demonstrates a connection between addiction and early experiences such as physical or emotional abuse, separation of parents, and parental incarceration. One study in the *Journal of*

Addictive Behaviors notes that for every increased point on the ACE scale (one point equals one traumatic event in childhood), there was an average of a 62 percent increase in the likelihood that a person would abuse prescription medication.

Connection

A sense of home is both treatment for addiction and a defense against it. From the rats of Rat Park to the returning Vietnam veterans, a positive change in environment had a dramatic effect on consumption patterns and addiction rates. We all desire a sense of connection, meaning, and place. When we don't have those things, we will seek them out or try to adapt to our environments.

While homelessness can sometimes be a result of a person's addictive behaviors, it can also create or exacerbate addictive behaviors. Helping individuals and families out of homelessness used to mean moving them through a series of steps: a temporary shelter, long-term shelter, temporary housing, and finally permanent housing. But advocates realized that extended periods of moving from place to place tend to exacerbate problems for individuals or families. All the stress of moving and uncertainty make it harder to do the kinds of things that would help someone get and keep permanent housing. Cities across the country have successfully implemented "housing first" programs, which seek to move people into a permanent home as quickly as possible while providing additional services.

A place to call home is a powerful prerequisite in helping people recover. In fact, outpatient treatment, for those who have a safe environment to call home, can be more effective than inpatient treatment. The loving support of a family and learning new coping skills and strategies in the environment in which you are living can help people maintain a newfound sobriety more easily.

Home is not just a place to live; it can include connections to one's culture. Alexander tells the story of the Alkali Lake Band in British Columbia, which went from a nearly 100 percent rate of alcoholism among its adult members to a 98 percent sobriety rate in seven short years. With leadership from the chief and his wife, the band recommitted themselves to old cultural practices, instituted communal principles of Alcoholics Anonymous, increased access to treatment, and worked with the local police to enforce alcohol prohibition on their lands. The Alkali do not just say that culture is a part of treatment; their motto is "Culture is treatment."[10]

An early acknowledgment of the way that social conditions can affect everyday decision-making appears in Proverbs 30:8-9: "Remove far from me falsehood and lying; give me neither poverty nor riches; feed me with the food that I need, or I shall be full, and deny you, and say, 'Who is the Lord?' or I shall be poor, and steal, and profane the name of my God."

In this passage, the writer acknowledges his own weaknesses—that if he were in different circumstances, he might do things differently. The writer does not want to be poor, because he knows that desperation might drive him to do things that he wouldn't otherwise do.

The writer of Proverbs also cites the problems that can come with a lot of wealth. If having a house and abundant physical resources were enough to protect you from addiction, then you'd never see the same celebrity both on *MTV Cribs* and in the tabloids heading off to rehab. One implication of the spread of the opioid crisis in middle-class and wealthy communities is that a large house in the suburbs may be more like a dull and isolating Skinner box than we had previously wanted to admit.

Each of us finds ourselves in a world not entirely of our own choosing. We come with a history, a context, resources, opportunities, and restrictions. We do not exist as beings divorced from our context. We are reminded over and over again that we are made up of the very stuff of the world around us. We are dust, and to dust we shall return. This is true in a material sense but also in a social and cultural sense.

Genesis contains two slightly different creation narratives. But constant in both accounts is the truth that God created the rest of the world before God created the humans. In other words, God did not make humans and *then* make them a home. God made a world and then drew human life out of that world. We are made up of and a part of the home in which we live. To understand ourselves, we must understand the homes we come from and the homes we make.

My home

Home is more than a house and deeper than the location of your residence. It is a place defined by the connections, relationships, and meaning that reside there. Always having had a home didn't guarantee that I would not get addicted, but when I did, it was a context and a grounding for recovery.

I fall into the fortunate third of Americans who, according to the ACE scale, experienced no major trauma under the age of eighteen. The loving and stable environment in which I was raised, and the marshaling of the resources of home in a time of crisis, was essential to my recovery.

It wasn't just my mom who came to my hospital bed but my dad who ran to the airport to catch a last-minute flight to be by my bedside. My older sister, Bethany, helped me laugh about the diaper and spent hours on the phone processing with me as I recovered. My younger sister, Abby, was studying to be a nurse and came into my hospital room with care and practical compassion. My brother told me about his wedding plans and gave me something to look forward to when he asked me to be his best man.

At the time, I was working for the nonprofit Sojourners. This organization continued to provide healthcare coverage and a salary and promised to hold my position until I was well enough to return. My boss, Jim Wallis, was one of the first people at the hospital when my procedure went wrong and raised the alarm about my deteriorating condition. Coworkers and friends arranged regular visits during my stay in the hospital and during my recovery afterward.

These facts are not tangential to my story of addiction and recovery; they are essential to it. What occurred around me shaped how I experienced this medical crisis. I think of the opening line of Charles Dickens's *David Copperfield*: "Whether I shall turn out to be the hero of my own life, or whether that station will be held by anybody else, these pages must show."

I can answer this question for you now, and maybe even save you a few chapters of reading. The hero of this story isn't me. The most important elements of my recovery were things and people beyond my control, gifts that were given to me.

No, I wasn't a bystander; my participation in my own recovery was required. But the takeaway from my story is not the scolding one that says, "If this guy recovered from an opioid addiction, others should be able to recover too." The lesson is that without the gifts of support, resources, and compassion of others, I might not have recovered.

Having a loving and stable home doesn't ensure protection against addiction. The fact that a child develops an addiction isn't necessarily an indictment of the parents. The environments that affect our lives are far more complex and powerful than just our close family and where we sleep at night. And one of the powerful forces that has fueled addiction is technology.

13

Technology

Alexander Wood, a physician from Scotland, is credited with the invention of the hypodermic needle. He believed that his invention would be a great leap forward in the medical sciences, and he was correct. It would allow for the delivery of a variety of treatments and medicines quickly and with accurate dosing, and it would be a great improvement over both oral ingestion and the anal suppositories popular at the time.

Wood also believed, as did many of his colleagues, that he had discovered the cure for "morphinism," or opioid addiction. Their understanding was that opium and morphine addiction was a disorder related to a literal appetite for the drug. If the drug was not eaten—that is, orally ingested—then no appetite would have the opportunity to form. The drug could be used to relieve pain and avoid the side effects of obsessive use.[1]

On this count Wood was wrong. Legend has it that his wife was the first to die from an intravenous opioid overdose.

This was not the first medical innovation intended to reduce addiction that backfired. German scientist Friedrich Sertüner was the first to isolate morphine from opium. Sertüner had performed many of the experiments on himself and was cautious about his invention, saying, "I consider it my duty to attract attention to the terrible effects of this new substance in order that calamity may be averted."[2]

But other doctors and drug manufacturers were not so cautious. It wasn't long before morphine was marketed as a cure for opium addiction.

By 1874, there was a growing public awareness that injected morphine was even more addictive than orally ingested opium. British pharmacist C. R. Adler Wright was searching for a non-habit-forming painkiller. He made a breakthrough in breaking down morphine even further when he isolated the molecule diacetylmorphine.

The chemical discovery remained relatively unnoticed until Bayer Laboratories developed the capacity to mass-produce it. The scientists believed it would make an excellent pain reliever and would be particularly effective for the treatment of tuberculosis and other lung diseases. While they had begun with the morphine molecule, they believed that breaking the chemical down further had removed any potentially addictive elements.

It was given the German name *heroisch*, meaning "heroic." In English it became known as heroin and was widely marketed as a cure for opium addiction.

Now a new crisis of technology is fueling overdose deaths.

Fentanyl

In the past few years, the percentage of the population misusing prescription opioids has decreased, and the percentage of people using heroin has only increased slightly. But the rate of overdose deaths has increased dramatically. Why?

One word: fentanyl.

Fentanyl and other synthetic opioids are so potent that users often don't know how much they are taking. The slightest miscalculation is a matter of life and death.

This chemical's potent nature initially meant that it could be administered through the skin via a patch. The release would happen over days and not hours, mitigating the highs and lows that often accompany taking pain pills. The hope was to effectively treat severe pain (often among those who had developed a tolerance to other medications) and minimize addiction.

The first wave of the opioid crisis began in the 1990s with prescription medication. By 2010, many users moved to heroin as prescription medications were restricted and their street cost grew. As Sam Quinones documents, innovative drug dealers made it as easy to order heroin as it was to order pizza. Ease of access and a ready market from those who had been introduced to opioids through prescription medications meant heroin usage and overdoses spiked.

Just a few years later, in 2013, fentanyl spread quickly and cheaply across the continent. Even as overall opioid use slowed, overdose deaths surged. The chemical involved (and now others like it) is simply far more dangerous than anything we've seen before.

The black market for drugs takes advantage of the technological advancements of increased potency and efficiency of distribution. But the medical advancements of decreased contamination and accuracy of dosing are left behind.

Opium has always been addictive. But the potency of the drugs today changes how we relate to them by speeding up the addictive process and making usage potentially fatal at any moment. The stronger the drug, the faster the feedback loop that leads to addiction. An opium addiction might have taken decades to descend to a deadly place a few hundred years ago; today it could take only a few years or months.

The story of technology is always mixed. What can bring relief from pain can be the very same thing that ends a life. Just as there is no "demon" drug, I do not think there is a "demon" technology. But this isn't to say that technology is neutral.

Our technological advancements shape how we live in the world. Ultimately, technology changes how we experience ourselves and relate to our own desires. We don't just change the world with our technology; we change ourselves by and with technology. And we are not only addicted to our technology; technology now facilitates addiction in ways that we are only beginning to discover.

Hidden costs

Technology, defined in one sense, encompasses all the many ways that we alter the world around us. Technology has revolutionized how we eat, the shelters in which we live, how we get from place to place, and the ways that we communicate with each other. Technology is a means to an end.

However, German philosopher Martin Heidegger wrote that technology can conceal as much as it reveals. A new technology can change how we view ourselves, others, and the world. Some of these changes are obvious, but many of them are hidden. Heidegger wrote: "Everywhere we remain unfree and chained to technology, whether we passionately affirm or deny it. But we are delivered over to it in the worst possible way when we regard it as something neutral; for this conception of it, to which today we particularly like to do homage, makes us utterly blind to the essence of technology."[3]

We might not even be aware of the ways that our technology changes us until we are changed. We might not notice our dependence on it until it is suddenly gone. We might start off using a technology and not be aware of the ways that it begins to use us. The freedom it initially supplies soon becomes a bondage.

Medical technologies, including pharmacological innovations, have transformed how we live and how long we live. While they have opened up new worlds of possibility and opportunity, they can make us forget our own fragility and lead us into temptations we've not known before.

Technology can also break down previous barriers we might have experienced to potential addictions. Compulsive sexual behavior that continues despite harmful consequences to one-self and others certainly isn't new; just read Augustine's *Confessions* for a second-century example. But these sorts of behaviors have had cultural, moral, and legal restrictions that often limit the level and the extent of the sexual addiction. Technology has slowly eroded these restrictions, first with the rise of the camera, then the video camera, and the Internet, and finally the cell phone. Online access to pornography now enables a behavior in a way that just didn't exist a few decades ago.

The same is true with shopping. Buying stuff isn't new. Nor is the tendency for people to buy too much stuff or to buy things that they can't afford. But the ease and immediacy of shopping online and access to easy and immediate credit has increased the problem of shopping addiction.

The benefits of technology are often immediate and clear to us. But their downsides and dangers are often unexpected and might take years to emerge.

Andrew Griffiths, an early researcher on technological and behavioral addictions, published a 2011 review paper that analyzed over eighty-three different studies including 1.5 million participants. The review looked at the categories of gambling, love, sex, shopping, Internet, exercise, and work. The conclusion? Griffith writes that 41 percent of the population had suffered some sort of behavioral addiction in the past twelve months.[4]

"Behavioral addictions" are now an official diagnosis in the diagnostic manual used by therapists. What previously might have just been labeled abnormal, antisocial, immoral, or unwise behavior is increasingly understood and being treated through the framework of addiction. Researchers can now observe the remarkable similarities between the brain activity of people who are struggling with sex, gambling, or shopping addictions and that of those who are addicted to cocaine, heroin, or meth.

You don't always need brain scans to know that something other than normal decision-making patterns are at work. When some gamblers wear diapers to a casino to play slot machines uninterrupted by restroom breaks, and when teenagers experience physical withdrawal symptoms when unable to play an online game, you can see the addictive nature of technology.

Technology doesn't just facilitate our addictions; it can also be our addiction. Adam Alter, author of *Irresistible: The Rise of Addictive Technology and the Business of Keeping Us Hooked*, notes one study that indicates that up to 40 percent of the population has some sort of Internet-based addiction, whether it's email, gaming, social media, or porn. Another study suggests that 48 percent of university students qualified as "Internet addicts," with another 40 percent considered borderline.

These numbers indicate not simply amount of use but also self-reported levels of harm or decreased quality of life as a result of people's relationship with various Internet-related activities. That means that 88 percent of university students know they aren't in control of their Internet use or are concerned they might not be. In other words, the vast majority of us are using technology in ways that we believe are harmful to ourselves and others and we keep doing it anyway.

The technology that reveals a new world also conceals from individuals, through distraction and obsession, their own hopes, dreams, and goals. Technology that was supposed to increase human power and control in the world has made people feel powerless to control their behavior in relation to it.

Addicted to technology

So why is our technology so addictive? It facilitates all the key factors for behavioral addiction.

Adam Alter highlights six "ingredients" of behavioral addiction. Each one is exacerbated or made more accessible by technology. These ingredients are "compelling goals that are just beyond reach; irresistible and unpredictable positive feedback; a sense of incremental progress and improvement; tasks that become slowly more difficult over time; unresolved tensions that demand resolution; and strong social connections."[5] Let's look briefly at each one.

Goals are a part of life and are essential for survival. But never before have we had so many eminently trackable goals present to us—and almost always still out of reach. We might monitor our weight with an app connected to our bathroom scale in constant pursuit of dropping just a few more pounds. Or we might obsessively check our email just to "keep on top of things," even if we fail to respond to all the incoming messages. If the goal is too distant or hard to imagine accomplishing, we are less likely to pursue it. If the goal is too easy, it becomes meaningless and might not grab our attention. But technology can connect what seems like a meaningless goal and imbue it with meaning. Suddenly your small increase of points changes the color of your avatar, earns you a badge, or moves you up a couple of spots on a leader board of competitors across the world.

The second element—irresistible and unpredictable feedback—may seem counterintuitive. But take gambling as an example. Our learning systems function by relying on the fact that most of the time when we repeat an action, we slowly get better at it. The more we hone our skills, the more likely we are to get an increased benefit. But when we repeat an action and our results vary, it can ignite in us a desire to continue trying to improve even though the results are completely or almost entirely driven by chance.

The third element—incremental improvement—is mimicked in gambling machines. If you are playing slots, there is nothing under your control but hitting a button or pulling a lever. But it mimics an action of learning. It can make you think that you are doing something that gets you closer to that desired goal. Digital slot machines today are programmed to mimic near misses; these make players believe that they are very close to getting something right—when in fact there is nothing they can do to improve their chances of winning.

Right alongside that sense of progress is our fourth element: tasks that slowly become more difficult over time. These kinds of challenges have always been with us—whether it is graduating to the next grade in school, moving through a training program, or doing the increasingly complex task of the daily *New York Times* crossword puzzle.

One of the simplest but most compelling examples is the game of Tetris. Decades after its introduction, it is still played regularly and is a source of enjoyment and distraction for many. It is a game that begins so easily and slowly increases in challenge and complexity. It provides a perverse kind of motivation by removing all your successes from the screen while showing you every mistake and the very things you've left incomplete.

The fifth element is unresolved tension. Lack of resolution is the drive behind much binge watching, an increasingly common example of an addictive process. The mystery remains unresolved, the plotline is just not quite complete, the other shoe just hasn't quite dropped. As soon as we see a list of top ten anything, it sparks a desire to know each one, even if we had never considered before how to rank the haircuts of every boy band member of the past thirty years.

Finally, social connections matter. In our day-to-day lives, we are constantly looking for feedback from those around us about how they are receiving what we are doing or saying. We use this feedback to gauge or change our behavior according to the feedback.

Imagine a young teenager posting their first photo to a new social media account. They refresh the screen every few seconds to watch the reactions and comments pour in. Every instance of positive feedback is sending another small hit of dopamine to their brain. The next day they do the same and revel in the feedback. The day after that, the whole cycle repeats itself. An entire week goes by, and each time the positive reactions grow.

But a week later, the teen posts a photo, and it only receives a handful of likes and one comment. The reactions are only a fraction of what they had been before. The teen begins to fret and obsess about what went wrong. They can't stop thinking about why that photo didn't receive the feedback the others had. What do they need to do to get that kind of feedback again?

Feedback that was once exciting becomes boring. A constant drive for more positive feedback dominates the day. What was once a tool for sharing one's life becomes the obsession. Life then becomes the tool used to feed the world of digital affirmation.

That final element might be the most dangerous of all. Technology provides a surface-level answer to the deep need for human relationship. The constant feedback from our digital networks is close to, but not quite the same as, our daily social interactions. It mimics, but does not fulfill, our desire for connection. In this way, we experience the desire for low-level signs of approval from a wide array of social contacts over and over, again and again.

Serenity Prayer

At the heart of any experience of Alcoholics Anonymous is the recitation of the Serenity Prayer, by Reinhold Niebuhr: "God, grant me the serenity to accept the things I cannot change, the courage to change the things I can, and the wisdom to know the difference."

This is a reminder for all of us that we are on both an active and a passive journey. There are things in life that make us angry or sad or cause pain that we have no control over. But we will always have a choice about how we accept or do not accept those things.

Descartes, in his *Discourse on Method*, wrote, "Always to master myself rather than fortune, and change my desires rather than changing how things stand in the world." At least part of our happiness rests on learning to change our responses to the world around us rather than changing the world.

When you expect to control the things that are external to you, you set yourself up for disappointment and frustration. Contentment is most within our grasp, Descartes said, when we "shan't want to be healthy when we are ill, free when imprisoned, any more than we now want to have bodies as hard as diamonds or wings that fly like birds."[6]

Technology makes this harder.

When Descartes was writing those words about health, the average life expectancy was close to forty. The idea of humans flying was fanciful, and now it is commonplace. The capacity of our technology and the efficiency of our economy has meant a dramatic change in how often we are able to control external circumstances. For most of human history, this level of control would have been considered not just a luxury, but impossible.

Those of us with privilege are now habituated to a level of consistent external control of our environment. This means that an internal state of acceptance when we can't satisfy our desires or needs is even harder to find. It wasn't that long ago that calling a cab meant at least a twenty-minute wait and maybe an hour. Today, thanks to ride-sharing services, I get frustrated if a ride isn't available to me in five minutes or less.

Our ability to know what is actually within our control and what is not begins to blur. Technology conceals itself; we forget that it is even present in our lives, that we are accessing information not through the capacity of our intellect but through the assistance of technology.

Technology is one of the powerful forces shaping how and why we get addicted. We have, because of technology, control over our environments and bodies in ways we never have had before. But this increased control in some areas means a loss of control in others. While addiction is characterized by a loss of control, it often begins in our attempts to gain control.

14

Control

The word *addiction* comes from the Latin word *addictus*. It is a combination of the prefix *ad-*, meaning "to" or "toward," and the verb *dīcere*, meaning "to say" or "to pronounce." In Roman times, *addictus* was the technical designation for a person who had been given over by a court into slavery.

For a person to become an *addictus* in Roman times required three separate people: the person being enslaved, the master, and the judge who made the pronouncement. In addiction, these lines are blurred. "Addiction robs one of oneself," Francis Seeburger writes. "It deprives one of the ownership of one's own life. That life ceases to be 'one's own' and becomes nothing more than an expression of the underlying addiction."[1]

A substance or behavior, which once was a tool to accomplish a specific end or a goal, turns out to be the master. It is not long before addiction is experienced not through the use of a substance but through the sense of being used by the substance. Instead of a judge handing out a sentence, we unwittingly hand over our freedom ourselves.

If we lose self-control, we lose control of the self, and it isn't long before the self is lost.

Addiction can come through a desire to control ourselves, our lives, and the world around us. And it can come through providing relief from the hurts we suffer when control has been taken away from us. Addiction will mimic whatever it is in your life that you believe you lack.

Regain control

When I was lying in my hospital bed, there was very little in my life that I felt I could control. The one thing that I knew I had consistent agency to do, and that would get a consistent outcome, was to push the button every fifteen minutes that released another small trickle of hydromorphone into my veins.

Back home after my hospital stay, my choices and control were still terribly limited. I could choose between movies, TV shows, and books. One of the few things I could do, and that allowed me to have control over how I felt, was taking more pain pills.

Taking pills also helped me wrest control back from the thing that had taken so much away from me: pain. When it feels like most of your life is out of your control, and then you discover something that makes you feel in control, you will cling to it.

Marc Lewis, a developmental neuroscientist and author of *The Biology of Desire*, profiles a man he calls Brian, describing the early stages of his addiction to cocaine that eventually turned into a meth addiction. Lewis writes, "He didn't love the feeling of coke, but he found it useful. It also helped him feel more present, more connected, when talking with his clients. It helped him work well into the night. There was too much work to finish in an eight-hour day."[2]

Lewis also tells the story of a woman he calls Alice and her struggle with anorexia. We tend to think about anorexia as the ultimate exercise of self-control. It epitomizes the ability to delay gratification and to put a long-term concern over a short-term pleasure. "Yet anorexia and addiction are as similar as twin sisters," writes Lewis. "Neither anorexics nor drug addicts exercise top-down control when it comes to the behaviour that harms them."[3] Alice, Lewis notes, lost her control to not starve herself. The way she exercised and approached food was no longer a simple free choice but a compulsive behavior.

The parts of our brain that misfire with alcohol and drug addiction go haywire in similar ways with anorexia, bulimia, and compulsive eating. The desire to be in control can mean losing control.[4]

How free?

I reached for pain medicine as a means of control but also as a way to ease my anxiety about my life being out of control.

Neuroscientist and addiction researcher Carl Hart describes in his book *High Price* the ways he saw the crack epidemic affecting the low-income Black neighborhood in which he grew up. Politicians and the media made those who were addicted to crack cocaine sound like inhuman monsters no longer capable of any rational thought, and hinted that the only hope for society was in locking everyone up. Hart knew from experience this wasn't right, but wanted to demonstrate it in his research as well.

He describes a series of experiments in which he offered those already addicted to cocaine a choice between cocaine and cash. It didn't take much economic incentive, even for those in the thrall of a deep addiction, to choose the money instead of the drugs.

Even if they did ultimately use the money to buy drugs, Hart argues, this choice still shows a rational and deliberative thought process to delay gratification of drug use in exchange for a monetary reward. Those who were addicted were look-ing to restore a sense of control over their lives. An offer of money was another way to fill that need. Hart notes that many people who are addicted, especially when they are low income, don't have a lot of "alternative reinforcers" in their life. The positive reinforcement the drugs provide is more consistent than other forms of potential feedback. The drugs that are available to them are often the cheapest sources of pleasure (and thus motivation) around.

Does this mean that a simple monetary incentive would allow everyone to just up and quit? No. Does it mean that anyone who is addicted just needs to try harder? No. What this does demonstrate is that the opportunities we as a society choose to offer or restrict for those who are suffering addictions matter. The harder we make it for people who have struggled with addiction to create a new and meaningful life, the less likely they are to do it.

Addiction can narrow our field of vision and limit the amount of new information we take in. Addiction can skew our capacity to weigh the trade-offs between short-term reward and long-term cost. These sorts of deliberations are things that humans are notoriously bad at anyway, and addiction can make it worse.

How does this look in practice?

A program in Seattle called Law Enforcement Assisted Diversion, or LEAD, has demonstrated the power of increasing meaningful choice for those struggling with addiction. The program targets those with long-standing addictions and a history of small crimes and misdemeanors. The folks who are part of the program typically have been arrested dozens of times in the past. They have lost control over their own lives.

Instead of receiving a court date and jail time, consistent offenders are asked what their goals are. These dreams are not dangled out in front of people like a carrot, only achievable if they stop using drugs. Instead, the person is immediately helped to take that first step. They might be given a job or an apartment, and they might be provided counseling services or connected to a medically assisted treatment program.

"Everyone has goals," says one of the social workers involved in the program. "I guarantee you once you work towards those goals and a couple of things come to fruition, you'll come back and say, 'I want to deal with my addiction.'"[5]

The Seattle program is not a magic fix, but participants have a 58 percent lower chance of rearrest than those in a similar demographic who were not chosen to participate. In restoring a sense of autonomy and control over one area of life, many people are able to begin exercising control in more areas of their lives.

The forces at work in the world that increase or decrease our own autonomy can have profound effects on the kind of solutions we seek. It is little wonder that those who think that their lives are beyond their control grasp for a way to regain control or achieve a control that they never had.

Sometimes we need to be reminded of who we are before we forget.

Forgetting

One of the attractions of addictive substances, and in some ways of addiction itself, is that if your life feels out of control, addiction offers you a moment to forget about that reality. But that offer comes with a steep price: forgetting.

One of the greatest tricks addiction plays is making you forget who you are and who you are not. When Odysseus and his men arrived on the island of the "lotus-eaters," they faced this dilemma. Odysseus sent out scouts who didn't return. When he found them, he realized that while the people of this island did not wish to kill or capture them, as many others they encountered did, there was a new danger on this island. The inhabitants had offered his men flowers (assumed today to be modeled after the poppy) that made any who ate them forget

their fears, their sorrows, and their homes. And although the
men on the ship were hungry, Odysseus brought the scouts
back kicking and screaming. He knew that if the men forgot
their homes, they would forget themselves and never finish
their journey.

The men were hungry, tired, and beleaguered. Their world
was out of control. While they longed for the rest and comfort
of their homes, the island of the lotus-eaters seemed to offer
the next best thing: forgetting about both their problems and
a seemingly impossible goal all at once.

Addiction functions in our brains by corrupting the natural processes by which we learn. In our lives more broadly,
addiction mimics a journey of self-discovery and growth. It
promises similar things that we find when we do the difficult
work of discovering who we are.

But instead of losing who we once thought we were and
discovering a deeper and truer sense of ourselves, we begin
to fall asleep. We start to forget. Instead of our concerns,
cares, and desires widening out in a way that connects us with
others and the world around us, we become closed off. Our
vision narrows.

The temptation is to numb ourselves, to live life in a trance,
or to fall asleep. Our pain demands a response. It will grab for
anything that seems to offer relief. In our addictions, we reach
for those things that provide an answer, even an incomplete
one. In our desire to control our pain, we lose control.

Again, this desire to forget is not an entirely bad one. It
mimics, in some ways, experiences many of us seek. For a religious person, it might be called an ecstatic or mystical experience, in which you forget your earthly concerns for a time
and feel directly connected with God or creation. For artists
and athletes it might be a sense of flow, in which the rest of the
world fades away while you are wholly engrossed in the joy of
the task before you.

A relatively new area of study concerns the "default mode network" in our brains. Neuroscientists realized that brain activity doesn't stop when we aren't actively working on a task or thinking through a problem; it just shifts gears. The default mode network is made up of the parts of our brain and the pathways between them that are activated when we are daydreaming, thinking about the future, remembering the past, rehearsing a conversation, or engaging in introspection.

An overactive default mode network is what we experience late at night when we can't fall asleep and we can't stop feeling anxious about an argument we had with a coworker or a bill that we're not sure how we will pay. It represents a part of our conscious thought that can sometimes feel out of control. Faulty functioning of this network is connected to anxiety, depression, and even addiction.

When we become so engaged in an activity or focused on an object of desire, this default mode network quiets down to a place in which we, at least momentarily, forget ourselves. Some research indicates that even a temporary reset of the default mode network can be highly effective in helping people get beyond all destructive addictions and patterns.

The apostle Paul seemed to have moments like this, and described himself as "it is no longer I who live, but it is Christ who lives in me" (Galatians 2:20). Thomas Merton's well-known revelation in *Conjectures of a Guilty Bystander* discloses a similar feeling: "In Louisville, at the corner of Fourth and Walnut, in the center of the shopping district, I was suddenly overwhelmed with the realization that I loved all those people, that they were mine and I theirs, that we could not be alien to one another even though we were total strangers. . . . There is no way of telling people that they are all walking around shining like the sun."[6]

Paul, far from describing his oneness with the Christ as debilitating, describes it as an ultimate form of freedom.

Merton is euphoric in his description of feeling a connection with everything and everyone around him. The loss of self, and the loss of control that comes with it, represents an ultimate kind of freedom in these passages. The feeling is intoxicating. Ralph Waldo Emerson warns that the feelings brought on by the use of opium or alcohol are dangerous precisely because they "ape in some manner these flames and generosities of the heart."[7]

Addiction is dangerous because of the ways that we lose self-control, in the traditional sense. But it is also dangerous because there are ways that a true freedom rests in a forgetting of ourselves. And nothing mimics that experience quite as well, at least for a while, as substances and behaviors that can prove addictive. The very reason some of these substances are addictive is their capacity to allow us to forget ourselves.

Addiction can stem from a desire to have control and a desire to forget the struggle of circumstances when we are not in control. But the question remains: Do people have control over their addictions? Is addiction a choice?

which in essence brings one further away from the true nature" as a living child of God.

15
Choice

No matter how bad things got in the hospital, I always believed I still had a choice.

In the first few weeks of my stay in the hospital, I could do very little. I lay in bed and was. Whatever I had been, I continued to be. The only changes were the additions and subtractions my illness brought. My decisions were confined to the spaces I controlled, and I controlled little except the button that allowed the pain medicine to flow.

My first big move was out of my bed and to a recliner a few feet away. The next was to abandon the diapers and bedpan and walk to the bathroom. Soon I could make halting steps out the door and into the hall. Each step hurt like the last. Each movement of my legs, dropping of my feet, and clutching of the pole with my hand was a conscious act. I focused on putting one foot in front of the other and set my eyes on the next door down. It was time to relearn what had once been habit.

I couldn't make it to the end of the hall the first time I tried. It was two, maybe three, attempts later when I finally made it all the way down to some couches. Tears welled up and filled my eyes. I tried to breathe deeply as I watched the cars below go by below.

For nearly an hour I sat on that couch, trying to build the strength and will to make the return walk to my room. Finally, I made a choice. I put one hand on the arm of the couch, wrapped the other around the IV pole, and slowly pulled myself up, I knew that this choice was mine. I looked down the hall, locked my eyes on the distant door of my room, and knew that this first step—and each after it—would be mine as well.

What I didn't know

Why don't people just choose to get better?

It is easy to imagine that, in order to recover from addiction, a person goes through a process like what I did as I chose to stand up and walk back down the hall to my room. Recovery is difficult, and a struggle, but ultimately a choice, right? If a person keeps on making the right choice, then recovery will be achieved.

In this view—of recovery as a conscious choice—I could choose to fight and recover and return to life outside the hospital and overcome my addiction one step at a time. There is some truth to this view. Those who have overcome their addictions might live for years, or maybe the rest of their lives, "one day at a time." Every day they choose to choose. They take one step, and then another, and then another.

But at the same time, this isn't the entire picture. In fact, if we stop here, we miss so much that is happening beneath the surface.

What I didn't know that day, as I rested at the end of that hospital hall, was that a pseudocyst—a collection of enzymes and other fluids in my pancreas—was quietly forming. Physical forces already set in motion were determining the direction of my life.

I had imagined myself, through the force of my own will, taking one step after the next toward recovery. Through summoning a deep inner strength, I believed I would overcome. I believed I could beat my illness, and I believed that my trip to the end of the hall and back was a metaphor for all recovery. I would take one step at a time, and one step at a time I would get better.

But the irony of that day is this: I wasn't getting better. I was actually getting worse. The vision I had of myself willing my own recovery was an illusion. My doctors would discharge me a few weeks later to a rehab facility—only to readmit me to the hospital a few days after that. My eyes would jaundice, I would spike a fever, my pseudocyst would burst, and my mother would cry at my bedside. The doctors would try one last procedure, and my father would catch the next flight, hoping to make it to my hospital room before it was too late.

Was my "choice" just an illusion? All this just evidence of a biological determinism? The things that I think are an exercise of my free will are actually just expressions of biological and physiological cause and effect. Does everything we covered in the last chapter represent a complex series of dominoes set to fall since the origin of the universe? Is addiction a predetermined disease or a condition beyond our control? Or is it a choice that we make to become addicted and a choice we must make to overcome?

In the world of philosophy, these questions have often been defined as a battle between free will and determinism. Free will emphasizes our capacity for choice. Determinism follows the logic of cause and effect; every action is a result of previous actions that were put into motion at the beginning of time. If we truly have free will, then nothing can really be "determined." But if everything is determined, free will is only an illusion.

One side had to be right and the other wrong. The debate seems intractable. But Kent Dunnington, in his book *Addiction and Virtue*, writes, "The false dichotomy arises from a failure or an inability to conceive of a genuine space between compulsion and choice, between, in philosophical terms, determinism and voluntarism."[1]

A school of thought called "compatibilism" has forged a middle ground. Why do we sometimes believe that we are in complete control of our actions and other times that someone else is calling the shots? Because that is what is happening. Our actions are never really completely free or completely determined but often somewhere in between. Free will helps us understand some situations and determinism will be helpful in others.

The truth about addiction is found not in swinging to either extreme but in understanding the dynamic tension and interplay between the different ends of this spectrum. One kind of action that falls into this space in between is quite common: they are called habits.

Habit

Before addiction was addiction, the primary word to describe consistent use of a substance like cocaine or opium was the word *habit*. Today, habit and addiction have been broken off as distinct phenomena. But the fact that they share this common heritage is indicative of how closely they are related.

Dunnington defines habit as "a relatively permanent acquired modification of a person that enables the person, when provoked by the relevant stimulus, to act consistently, successfully and with ease with respect to some objective."[2]

Habits are a kind of deep learning that include both the conscious and the automatic parts of our brain. As habits are formed, things that used to require conscious thought become automatic. This level of learning allows us to build on these behaviors and engage in other more complex behaviors or think about other things at the same time.

We might say we "choose" to walk to the store—but we wouldn't say that we "chose" to take each step to the store.

The day I walked down a hallway for the first time in almost a month stood out so starkly in my memory because it *did* take a conscious act of the will to take each step. My habit of walking had been temporarily disrupted, so doing it again was exhausting not only physically but mentally and emotionally as well.

Habits are, by their nature, difficult to break. If it isn't hard to change, then it never qualified as a habit at all. This isn't the brain just being difficult. The deep learning that occurs that makes a habit hard to break is also what allows us to accomplish complex functions without having to consciously think through each step of the process. Habits save our energy and attention.

The development of a habit is that movement from a repetitive behavior or disposition to something that becomes second nature. Once we develop a habit, it becomes increasingly difficult to distinguish between the habit and the core of who we are.

Habits are actions somewhere in between voluntary and involuntary. Thomas Aquinas, the 13th century theologian, wrote extensively on moral habits, called virtues, and said, "He who throws a stone is able not to throw it; however once he has thrown the stone he has not the power to take back the throwing. . . . Hence we say that men are voluntarily unjust and incontinent, although, after they have become such, it is no longer within their power to cease being unjust or incontinent immediately, but great effort and practice are required."[3]

Addiction, in this sense, can be understood as a stone that cannot be un-thrown. Those who are suffering a severe addiction threw that stone without knowing it might cause an avalanche. It is, to take another analogy of Aquinas's, like a man who ate bad food and got sick. True, he should have avoided the food in the first place; but now that he has eaten, "it is no longer in his power not to be sick."[4]

If all addiction begins in some kind of pain—whether conscious or unconscious, physical or emotional or spiritual—we need to take these analogies a step further. What if that stone was thrown not out of malevolence or even ignorance but out of self-defense? What if the food that caused the illness was eaten not out of gluttony but because of a devastating hunger?

Body knowledge

Habits, then, are a kind of embodied knowledge. Our bodies are constantly learning from our actions and our environments. At least some of this learning is happening without our conscious or reflective awareness. Habits are what we develop to get the automatic self and the conscious self working together. They are the pathways of communication to make sure the different decision-making centers in our bodies are cooperating.

We need to engage our entire selves in this process. Christiane Northrup, an author and women's health specialist, writes, "Not only do our physical organs contain receptor sites for the neurochemicals of thought and emotion, our organs and immune systems *can themselves manufacture these same chemicals*. What this means is that our entire body feels and expresses emotion—all parts of us 'think' and 'feel.' . . . *The mind is located throughout the body*."[5]

Or as Candace Pert, sometimes known as the mother of psychoneuroimmunology, puts it, "the body is the outward manifestation of the mind."[6]

Creating new and better habits requires an awareness of the parts of ourselves that can serve a particular purpose but might easily go awry. In the natural world, deer are a good example. The instinct for a deer, when it senses an unknown threat, is to observe the threat and evaluate. The speed at which a deer can run, for most of its history as a species, has been just about as fast as its most common predators.

Thus pausing for a moment to evaluate the situation before running was a helpful and strategic behavior over millennia. With the rise of the bow and arrow and then firearms, however, the pause became a boon for the hunter who took that moment to take aim.

In his book *The Body Keeps the Score*, Besser van der Kolk details all the many ways that our bodies hold knowledge of past hurts and traumas. Our bodies respond with high levels of stress hormones, priming us to fight or flee. But living at that level of stress can increase the incidence of all sorts of health problems, including diabetes, heart disease, and addiction.

Our bodies hold a great deal of knowledge that influences our health and well-being. It is not a question of *if* this knowledge changes us but whether we are conscious of *how*. The choices we make are a dynamic interplay between what we often define as "free will" and what is "determined." We can address underlying physical causes and our conscious decision-making at the same time.

This is why medication assisted treatment (MAT) is so important. MAT is a general term for combining various kinds of therapy with medication. The most common drugs used in MAT are buprenorphine, naltrexone, and methadone.

Methadone, the most widely known, is an opioid-based medication that can reduce cravings and withdrawal symptoms for those with an opioid addiction. Naltrexone blocks the opioid receptors so that even if you do take an opioid, you won't feel the effects. Buprenorphine does a little of both, by simultaneously blocking other opioids and mimicking them, thereby reducing cravings and withdrawal symptoms.

The combination of therapy and medication is highly effective. One British study found that patients who received only psychological support "appear to be at greater risk of fatal opioid poisoning," nearly double the rate, than those who received MAT.[7] The evidence continues to mount that this kind of holistic treatment is the gold standard for opioid recovery. Still, access to MAT is relatively limited.

Critics often point to the possibility that both methadone and buprenorphine can be abused, which is true. Some also argue that those using MAT are just trading one drug addiction for another drug addiction. Or that MAT is nothing but a "crutch." MAT *is* a crutch. That is exactly why access is so important. A crutch is a critical tool if you are trying to heal a broken foot. MAT is important if you are trying to let the brain heal from the damage that addiction has caused. The medications directly address some of the physical aspects of addiction while not ignoring the psychological.

Can crutches be abused? Yes. But that doesn't mean we shouldn't make them available. Can crutches cause problems if improperly used or used for too long? They sure can. But that doesn't mean a physical therapist is going to tell someone after a knee surgery to just push through the pain and walk again.

Every experience of addiction is different and that means every story of recovery will be too. Some people recover and thrive without medication, but that doesn't mean everyone will or should be expected to.

Habit Forming

Sleep aids and pain medicines often carry the warning "Caution: Habit Forming." This is to let the user know that the chemicals included have been known to create habits, or addictions, in other users.

Habits are also forming in the sense that they form us. Habits have the power to shape and change who we are and how we experience the world. Aristotle and a whole school of thinkers, often referred to as virtue ethics theorists, focus on the formation of habit. These theorists believe that your capacity to know right from wrong isn't enough; you need to develop habits that prepare you for different situations. Then you will have the embodied knowledge to do the right thing even if you don't have time to reflect on what the right thing might be.

My grandma thought it was crucial that I learn to hold the door open for others. More than once as a kid, I'd walk into a store in front of my grandmother . . . only to look back and see her standing outside the door, looking at me with her arms crossed. She'd stand there until I came back and opened the door for her.

The strength and effort it takes to open a door are minimal. Most people, most of the time, can do it just fine on their own. Holding the door open for another person is important not because holding the door is such a great thing; it is important because it helps you develop the *habit* of doing it for the moments it really matters. What's the best way to ensure that you hold the door open for someone who might have a hard time opening it, or for someone who is carrying bags of groceries? By getting into the habit of holding the door open for everyone—even people who can do it for themselves.

Holding the door can also be an exercise in being aware of the space you are in and the people who are around you. One of the best ways to create the habit of awareness of the needs of others is to create regular moments in which you are checking in with the people around you. Opening the door can be a habituation of consideration for others.

Habits shape and change who we are and what we desire. They are a critical part of how we are formed—which is why it can be so devastating when our habits go wrong.

The cancer of habits

Addiction is like a cancer of our habits.

Our cells naturally grow and duplicate. Cell replication is essential to our life and health. But this natural and good process can go wrong. Sometimes it is simple and harmless, resulting in a small mole. Sometimes small polyps or precancerous growths develop but remain benign.

Other times those growths stay small and unobtrusive for years . . . until they aren't. They might go unnoticed and without symptoms for decades, only to grow out of control, spread, and become life-threatening. Some people go from being cancer-free to having an aggressive tumor that is deadly in a matter of months.

The same is true with our habits. They are necessary for our growth and survival. They perform vital functions and are often helpful. Sometimes they grow fast but in benign ways, like an addiction to coffee. Other times the negative consequences can slowly manifest over the course of decades. A food addiction developed early in life, for example, might only become life-threatening years later with a heart attack.

Some people smoke regularly and drink more than is recommended their entire lives without significant health damage or apparent negative consequences for their career, financial situation, or close relationships. Another person might drink heavily for decades without apparent consequences—only to suddenly lose their job one day and then find themselves in a quickly worsening spiral. Others will look back and see an immediate downward spiral from the moment of their first drink or time using a drug.

Habits can help us gain control of our emotions and shape our desires. They can also spiral away from us and make us lose control. These moments—when our ideals about who we are and who we want to be don't line up with our actions— lead to another experience we all know well: denial.

16

Denial

Did I know? Before the doctor told me, did I know I was addicted?

I've thought about this question a lot. In some ways, the possibility that I was addicted was not foreign to me. Multiple doctors had told me that I didn't really need the pain medicine; I just wanted it. But each time it turned out that they had missed a complication. Each time my pain proved to be severe and real.

At the same time, the possibility that I was addicted struck me as credible. I knew it was possible. I've never been known as or prided myself on being a person with a great deal of self-control. Both sides of my family had histories of alcoholism. Addiction, I knew, was well within a realm of possibility.

But being aware of the possibility that I was addicted didn't mean I had the capacity to see it when it was happening. When I look back now, I wonder. Even if I didn't think it was addiction, did I know, at some level, that something wasn't right and needed to change?

I really don't know. If I *did* know I was addicted, I was still lying to myself or at least trying to hide the truth (and was doing a pretty good job of it). But if I knew, really knew, then how was it possible to lie to myself? Telling a lie requires one person to deceive and another person to be deceived, right?

How is it possible to be both deceiver and deceived at the same time?

David

Choosing to lie isn't the only way that we fail to tell the truth. Addiction is dangerous not simply because of the lies that we consciously tell but because of the lies that we have come to believe ourselves.

We often say we wear different hats or play different roles. Sometimes this capacity to be different selves in different situations is a survival and defensive mechanism. If you go to a job where you regularly feel demeaned and dismissed, you might separate that self from your home life so that you don't let the discouragement you feel interfere with how you are raising your children. Or, if you are a victim of trauma, you might disassociate from the moment of that trauma because it is too much to bear. Compartmentalization allows you to wait until a time when you feel safe and secure to begin processing the traumatic event.

What can be a behavior of self-protection, however, is also at the heart of hypocrisy. It is why even those who perpetrate terrible violence in one part of their life might go home and think of themselves as a "good guy."

In 2 Samuel, the prophet Nathan came to King David and told him a story. There was a man, Nathan explained, who was quite poor but had a prized lamb. This lamb grew up with the man's children, ate with them, and even drank from his cup. There was a rich man, with many flocks of sheep and herds of animals. When a visitor came to the rich man's house, the rich man didn't want to give up any of his animals. Instead, he stole the lamb from the poor man and prepared it as dinner for his guests.

Nathan told King David this story soon after what many scholars of Scripture now refer to as the rape of Bathsheba.

From his roof, King David saw Bathsheba bathing, sent for her, and slept with her. But her husband, Uriah, was off at war. When David learned of the resulting pregnancy, he called Uriah back to his palace. David tried to get Uriah to go home and spend time with his wife so that the paternity of the child would not be questioned. When that didn't work, he tried to get Uriah drunk and hoped that would get him to return to his wife.

When the plan failed, David had a commander send Uriah into the heat of a battle, where he would almost certainly be killed. This plan worked. David then took Bathsheba as his wife.

When David heard Nathan's story of the man who stole the lamb, "David's anger was greatly kindled against the man. He said to Nathan, 'As the Lord lives, the man who has done this deserves to die; he shall restore the lamb fourfold, because he did this thing, and because he had no pity'" (2 Samuel 12:5-6).

Nathan responded, "You are the man!"

In this account, David's disassociation was traumatic and deadly. Nathan's story showed that David knew the sort of thing he had done was terrible. It wasn't just information that he possessed but a viscerally held belief. David didn't hear the story as a removed moral judge and note that it was wrong. He reacted in anger. He wanted punishment and vengeance on behalf of the wronged.

David's self-deception was deep. But when confronted, he also demonstrated a deep desire to see justice done. He disassociated with the version of himself who raped a woman and then had her husband killed to cover up his crimes. He disassociated precisely because a part of him knew exactly how terrible these acts were.

Deception

Deceit is often motivated by a desire to get away with something. But deceiving yourself can emerge from something entirely different. Self-deception can be just as damaging as deceiving another, but it is sometimes prompted by a desire to be a better person than the one you are currently being. Instead of changing the behavior, you tell yourself a different story that lets you maintain your positive self-perception and continue acting the same way.

From one angle, this could be a sign of some hope: that is, people engaged in self-deception have a moral compass intact enough to know that what they are doing isn't right. Otherwise, the deception wouldn't be necessary. Then again, people engaged in self-deception are capable of attributing positive motivations to the bad thing they are doing. It isn't just that they are doing something wrong; they are telling themselves that they are only doing wrong because they want to do something right.

David might have told himself that sending his men to get Bathsheba was just a friendly invitation. But Bathsheba certainly knew that the refusal of a king's wish could end not only her life but the lives of everyone she loved.

When Bathsheba arrived, passing through the palace doors, walking by the armed guards, she probably shook with fear and uncertainty. David, comfortable in the surroundings he had grown used to, might have convinced himself that Bathsheba would simply feel flattered at the invitation. Perhaps he had even told himself that the purpose of the invitation was simply friendly and social.

We do not know the details of what happened between David and Bathsheba. But by today's standards, it was not anything close to consensual. It was the invitation of a king to a woman who was well aware that the man who had invited her would be willing to do everything necessary to get what he wanted.

Maybe David told himself it was still for the sake of Bathsheba. He would, after all, marry her as soon as her husband died. And this way she would be the widow of a hero and married to a king. If she had been found to be bearing a child from a man who was not her husband, she could have been killed by stoning.

Nathan understood that David was tied up in his own self-deceptions. David could no longer see clearly the immorality of his own actions. At the same time, Nathan understood that the self-deception did not necessarily indicate a moral hopelessness. Somewhere inside, David might still have had a sense of what was good, right, and just. David's self-deception also showed that he had a desire to be a good and just king. Other kings at the time wouldn't have even bothered with the deception. They thought of themselves as all-powerful, and they defined justice as whatever they willed it to be.

David's self-deception was thus simultaneously an opening for positive change and an even greater danger than if a king was simply an open tyrant. Those who continue in a self-deception are the ones Jesus called "whitewashed tombs": "beautiful on the outside but on the inside are full of the bones of the dead and everything unclean" (Matthew 23:27 NIV).

Our own standards

Helping a person overcome addiction is best achieved not by the imposition of an external moral standard but by helping the person define their own aspirations and providing the tools and strategies needed to accomplish them. We will look at this in more detail in chapter 19.

If I am ever confronted with a set of external standards and demands to live up to them, don't be surprised if I get defensive. I'll want to prove that *my* standards are the right ones, or that the other person is wrong about my life. This pretty well sums up my high school years and explains most of my detentions. Not too much has changed since.

What Nathan accomplishes with David is to draw out the standards that David purports to live by. He asks David what he believes the standards of justice should be. Instead of externally imposing a morality upon David, he calls David to honesty and reminds him of his own aspirations.

Our failures, when we do not address them honestly, cascade into a series of self-justifications. Those self-justifications then become codified into a new "moral" code, which is really just an excuse for prior failings.

Each choice we make to *not* address the initial failings requires a larger investment of self-justification to defend the previous actions. David had to continually justify his behavior with a new exercise of his power as the king. It was only the confrontation by Nathan, and David's subsequent repentance, that stopped this devolving process.

Confronting and dealing with our own self-deceptions are crucial steps toward healing. We might discover that the self-deception is rooted in a deep desire to be a better person than our behavior displays. Or we might find that there is a deeper and better version of ourselves that we have covered up and denied in an effort to conform to a culture that rejects all or part of who we are.

Bad Faith

Our addictions make promises they cannot keep. They mimic solutions as opposed to providing them. They are short-term solutions to long-term problems.

But it is important to remember that addictions do provide a kind of solution. While creating long-term disasters, they might be solving short-term problems. This is why our self-deceptions are so hard to shake: they contain an element of truth or serve some kind of purpose that is important to us. Once we are in the midst of them, they are hard to leave behind.

Philosopher Jean Paul Sartre called this self-deception "bad faith." It is the many ways that we deny something that is real and true about ourselves. Faith, as we'll explore later, requires receptivity to a new possibility. Bad faith shuts that down.

The way of bad faith is not always a conscious choice but often just the path of least resistance. Sartre writes, "One puts oneself in bad faith as one goes to sleep and one is in bad faith as one dreams. Once this mode of being has been realized, it is as difficult to get out of it as to wake oneself up."[1]

David functioned in bad faith throughout the story of Bathsheba. With each step of his deception, he refused to acknowledge what his actions indicated. The initial rape required a cover-up. The failed cover-up required a murder. Once a deception is set in motion, it tends to stay in motion except when acted upon by an equal or opposite force.

When the trance is finally broken, we need some sort of shaking awake. We need to be brought back to life from death.

The picture of those who have fallen asleep is present throughout the Gospels. Jesus tells his followers that his friend Lazarus is not dead but has "fallen asleep." He tells the story of the bridesmaids who "fall asleep" while waiting for the bridegroom. The disciples "fall asleep" in the garden of Gethsemane on the night Jesus is betrayed. And Paul, in Ephesians, says, "Sleeper, awake! Rise from the dead" (Ephesians 5:14).

To "fall asleep," in many traditions, is akin to death. To live in self-deception is to dwell in a state in which we are asleep to our lives and awake to our lies. The self-deception we are capable of can be even more harmful than if we didn't put up any pretenses at all.

Addiction always involves a level of deception. At first, these deceits may be small. It could be as simple as slowly increasing the size of your liquor pour while counting the same amount of drinks. Then it might be the deception of a friend or loved one, to whom you explain that yes, you like to drink after work, but only to unwind. Why would you mention that you put something extra in your coffee in the morning? That isn't really drinking; it's just helping you wake up and feel better.

It doesn't take long for these denials, deceits, or misdirections to feed themselves. They require more and more elaborate ruses to maintain themselves. Over time, the object of addiction and the entire framework constructed around the addiction picks up a kind of downward weight.

"Now we see through a glass, darkly; but then face to face," Paul wrote (1 Corinthians 13:12 KJV). The way we see the world and experience our lives is not completely transparent. We are always in the process of interpretation that is based on the lens we have or the stories we know. Addiction reorients our being and warps the meaning we find in the world. We already see through a glass darkly; addiction distorts that glass even more.

Addiction creates a narrowed view of the world, one in which new possibilities for freedom can be invisible. The very thing you need to escape from your addiction is one of the first things that addiction takes away from you: a vision for how life can be. "For it would have been better for us to serve the Egyptians than to die in the wilderness" (Exodus 14:12b): this statement of the Hebrew people, who had just been rescued from slavery, was not the truth. But it also was not intended to deceive. It discloses a way of viewing the world, and there were a lot of reasons, from the perspective of the recently freed people, to believe it. The evidence seemed to be on the side of those who were ready to return.

Only a few chapters later in Exodus, the "We'd have been better off in Egypt" complaint resurfaces again. It becomes a recurring theme throughout the Israelites' forty-year journey in the desert. That journey shows just how persistent those lies can be. Sometimes, self-deception takes generations to overcome.

If addiction were only fed by simple lies or deception, it would be easier to confront. But it functions in a reflexive spiral, in which small lies become deeply held beliefs. These beliefs begin to reflect back to the person a distorted view of themselves. The more distorted the view of the self becomes, the more distorted the view of the world.

The United States is now forty years into our collective denial of the depths of our own addictions and the rise of the overdose crisis. But the answer is not found in going back to Egypt. Hope is found in the meaning we can make for our future.

17

Meaning

Addiction does not represent a rejection of a good and moral life. Addiction often begins in the pursuit of a good life: of fulfillment, of belonging, of community, of friendship, of connection, of healing, of freedom, of wholeness, of peace, of happiness, of safety.

This idea might sound counterintuitive, but it's true. Yes, something, somewhere, goes wrong, but that doesn't mean that addiction is not, at root, a seeking after some sort of good.

If you have lived a life in pursuit of connection to others but haven't found it, the first substance you try that produces a facsimile of that experience might become the object of your addiction.

If you have been in pain and sought relief but never found it, the first thing that brings even a modicum of comfort might become the center of your addiction.

If you have sought a purpose above and beyond yourself and never been sure what it is that can fill that void, the first thing that grabs and pursues you with a craving for more just might become your all-encompassing addiction.

Addiction isn't dangerous because it never tells the truth. Addiction is dangerous because it only tells part of the truth. Addiction's power is how it mixes the truth and lies. The devil doesn't come with a pitchfork, hooves, and the smell of sulfur; the devil comes as an angel of light.

The experiences of a middle-aged white miner in West Virginia who is out of work in the year 2000, the life of a young Black man in Detroit in the 1990s, or of a middle-class woman in the 1890s would be dramatically different. My story is different from all of theirs. Still, we all would long for respect from those around us. We all want work that gives us meaning and purpose. Each of us wants autonomy and a sense that we control our own destinies. If we feel threatened or afraid, we grasp for whatever might make us feel safe or in control.

Each story is a search for a kind of transcendence. In each of us, there is a desire to live in a way that is more than just the life circumstance we've been given. We want to step outside of and beyond our day-to-day existence. We search for relief from pain and a way to fight back against the weight of acedia.

I didn't realize how true this was for me until I wrote this book.

Hymn of praise

I wrote tens of thousands of words in the months after my discharge from the hospital. Basically, I wrote a book that would never be published. Not once in those pages did I write the word *addiction*.

It was only after a year of research for this book that I went back and read what I had written. The warning signs of addiction were everywhere. Mingled throughout those chapters were these sorts of love songs to the pain medicine:

> I stared at the clear drop as it slowly gathered liquid to itself. Its pregnancy moved quickly and predictably. It started as a clear line of fluid before the small bump took form. There it grew as a protrusion gaining distinction

from its source. I could feel the latent energy ready to burst forth at the moment when gravity would overcome viscosity. All at once, the drop made a break from its plastic home above the tangled nest of clear plastic tubes and fell. It reveled in its moment between origin and destination where it was its own entity; free and separate from all surroundings. Then it was gone, sucked into the stream of all the other countless drops that made their way to my veins. My eyes returned to the place where the new drop would be born, already destined to leave its place of birth and join with my body.

I loved those drops. They had returned what peace and security they could afford into my life. Every fifteen minutes I knew I could press a button and hear the faint whir of electronics and know that the drip would become a flow and in a matter of seconds the warmth would spread throughout my body, my muscles would relax, and my head fall back into the pillow. That flow I could control, I could count on it. It was not a cure. I understood that. But in the absence of a liquid that could heal the source of my pain, the liquid that could make the pain bearable was the best lover I could ask for.

It was not just the relief of pain that I associated with the medicine, although that sort of negative reinforcement is powerful. It was also the positive associations I began to make with the substance. When you read addiction stories, memoirs, and poetry, there are often early ecstatic, religious, near beatific visions of love and beauty.

Samuel Taylor Coleridge, early in his own opium addiction, wrote:

In Xanadu did Kubla Khan
A stately pleasure-dome decree:
Where Alph, the sacred river, ran
Through caverns measureless to man
Down to a sunless sea.

His "vision in a dream. A fragment" ends with a drink of "the milk of Paradise," an oblique reference to the resin of the opium poppy.[1]

The Netflix documentary *Heroin(e)* follows three women battling the opioid crisis in Huntington, West Virginia. One of the women, a self-described "street missionary," focuses her religious zeal on helping women caught in addiction and sex work. After seeing a woman relapse again, the woman running the ministry asks her how the drug could have such a great draw over and over again.

The woman who relapsed answers, "I guess for you it would be kind of like kissing Jesus."

Meaning and ritual

The hook of opioids in my brain spread far beyond just the initial opioid receptors and a chemical dependency. It moved out into a place in which those chemical hooks created other pathways into the meaning centers of my brain.

Opioids became not just relief from pain but safety from danger. I was afraid of the pain. I took the pain medicine to put up a wall between me and the fear I felt when I was lying in the hospital bed, hearing doctors assign percentages to the likelihood of my survival. I took it to fend off the anxiety and dread I felt when family members gathered at my bedside with tears in their eyes.

Rituals are one of the ways that humans create, communicate, and pass on meaning. The prominence of rituals amid addiction is evident of the meaning an addiction holds, whether that meaning is explicit or unrealized.

Heroin users often have a complex ritual for preparation and injection of the drug. Smokers often find it so difficult to quit not just because of nicotine but because of the entire process of smoking. If nicotine addiction were just about the chemical, nicotine gum or patches would provide an easy solution. But they don't. Addiction might find its center in a chemical, but its grip is broader and deeper.

Addiction rituals become so powerful that some addicts will repeat the process even without the drug. Vancouver, British Columbia, once went through a short period in which the flow of heroin into the city nearly ceased. Dealers were desperate for supply, and users for a fix. Dealers cut the remaining heroin to contain less and less of any active substance. In some cases, the "drugs" contained no actual heroin at all. Even when many users became aware of this, however, they kept injecting. The ritual became so imbued with meaning that the process without the substance provided at least a small semblance of familiarity and relief.[2]

This does not mean those users were delusional; this simply demonstrates how deep the learning of addiction goes. For six months after I was discharged from the hospital, I couldn't eat a normal diet. While I was in the hospital I was kept NPO: a medical term for patients who are to receive nothing by mouth. All my nutrients were pumped into a PICC line, a sort of semi-permanent IV line to keep me alive.

Each day after I was discharged from the hospital, I had a complex ritual of setting up a pump system that would slowly deliver liquid and nutrients for the next twelve hours. Part of the process included "flushing my lines" with saline solution using a small syringe of salt water. This flush of liquid into my veins was completely benign, containing no medication at all. Still, with each push, I always felt a moment of euphoria and a sense of comfort.

The liquid injected through an IV or PICC line is typically at room temperature, a good twenty degrees Fahrenheit cooler than body temperature. The injection brings with it a tingling, cool sensation that spreads momentarily and then disappears. I still remember that feeling, which accompanied my first injection of morphine and then hydromorphone. Not only did the pain dull, but the anxiety rolled back from its high tide. The tension in my body started to dissipate. Amid my fear of a new medical diagnosis, I experienced great comfort and relief right after that chill ran up my arm. It was not just a medicine anymore but a savior.

Months after the last push of pain medicine into my veins, I was still pushing in that inert saline solution. Hundreds of injections later, I still felt a tingle of euphoria and a sense of comfort with each flush.

A placebo effect has an actual effect. Scientists have confirmed that placebos can trigger a release of endorphins, the body's natural pain reliever and anxiety reducer. I was not merely imagining the euphoria or conjuring up a sense of the pain being soothed; I was experiencing a true chemical change.[3]

I knew there was no pain medicine in that syringe. But that didn't stop the feeling. In my case, salt water mimicked the chemical effects of an opioid. The addiction was beyond the syringe, beyond the opioid molecule. It had settled into deep tracks well-worn in my brain.

Addicted to addiction

The great blessing and burden of our lives is the extent to which we have choice. The sad reality is that in much of our lives, we are not awake enough to know how much we are free. We often opt instead for the way of least resistance. Viktor Frankl, the Viennese psychologist and Holocaust survivor, understood humans as primarily driven by our "will to meaning." It is meaning and purpose that drives us to survive, push through suffering, or work to achieve our goals.

Addiction can occur not just because we become attached and focused on the object of our addiction but because we become addicted to being addicted. The constant awareness of the search for meaning and purpose can be as exhausting as it is exhilarating.

What addictions, both small and large, offer is a relief from this burden. Francis Seeburger suggests, "What addiction distracts me from is my own life. In such distraction, it relieves me of the burden of that life, of actually having to live it out, with all the uncertainty, boredom, routine, frustration, and disappointment that so often characterize even the most fortunate life."[4]

In this way, it is not just the object of our addiction that tempts us; it is the state of being addicted itself. Addiction is all the many ways that we fall asleep in the middle of our own lives. It is the many ways that we hand over the challenges of being and becoming to something that promises to shoulder this responsibility on our behalf.

Forces around us will always vie to take that freedom from us, with varying degrees of success. But the sad reality is that many of us are not coerced or forced into giving away this freedom. Instead, we freely hand it over.

"Addiction relieves me of the need to keep on searching for meaning in my life, the need to give my own life meaning through commitment, dedication, and daily perseverance," Seeburger writes. "Thanks to my addiction, the search is over, I no longer have to give my own life meaning. My addiction gives it meaning. My addiction is the meaning."[5]

At the heart of addiction is the loss of oneself. It is the handing over of responsibility for developing our own identity to the endless, ritualized repetition of one's addiction. The next step is always set, because every choice, every step, everything in one's possession is given over to the protection and pursuit of the addiction.

Spiritus

Spiritus contra spiritum. Psychoanalyst Carl Jung's now-famous formulation for the heart of the problem of alcoholism is a play on Latin words. *Spiritus contra spiritum*: spirit (alcohol) against spirit (of a human).

Jung did not write much about addiction during his career. But in a letter penned near the end of Jung's life, addressed to Alcoholics Anonymous cofounder Bill Wilson, Jung wrote about one of his former patients: "His craving for alcohol was the equivalent of . . . the spiritual thirst of our being for wholeness, expressed . . . as the union with God."[6]

Jung admitted to Wilson that throughout his career, he had been careful what he said publicly about addiction out of concern that his views would be ridiculed by colleagues in his field. Speaking of the need of a "spiritual awakening" to overcome alcoholism, for example, did not cohere with psychological trends at the time that dismissed religious belief. Jung did not want to sound as if, out of frustration with a lack of medical and scientific progress, he was throwing up his hands and saying, "Nothing else explains it; addiction must be spiritual!" Yet Jung intuited that addiction reflected some sort of grasping for deeper meaning.

In the theological realm, there is a problem called "god of the gaps." It notes that God, gods, or spirits are often posited as the answer for anything we don't understand. Why don't the crops grow? The gods are angry. Why did we win this battle? The gods are pleased. Why did this person get sick? She must have angered God. How will she get well? She must please God.

An idea of God that is posited every time we don't understand something is a pretty weak version of God. When your conception of God is based on an entity that fills in gaps of human knowledge, you end up with a moral and intellectual hazard. New information and research become constant threats. Religion then becomes a force holding back and standing in opposition to medical and scientific discovery.

There is a real concern among many professionals that progress in addiction treatment will be held back by religious belief: to paraphrase Jung, *spiritus contra scientiam*. Their fears are not entirely unfounded.

Both Christians and addiction treatment would benefit from a banishment of the "god of the gaps"—a concept of God available at our beck and call to explain all the unknowns. Sadly, recovery centers across the country are not always grounded in the best evidence of what actually helps. Instead, the focus is on a narrow, and sometimes harmful, view of spirituality that stands in opposition to medical advances. Instead of seeing that meaning is part of the problem, it can be seen as the only problem and ignore the biological and medical aspects of addiction.

Yet this doesn't mean that God, or AA's "higher power," or religion more broadly should be banished from addiction treatment. Religion, at its core, is about proposing value in the world and then establishing practices and relationships to bring about more of what is valued. It is through assignment of value and achievement of that value that we create and discover meaning. It is exactly because religion has such a deeper power to heal that it also has the capacity to cause such great harm.

What if what we mean when we say "religion" is one aspect of what it means to be human? Each of us, through our actions, displays that we value some things over other things. The things we value might be related to traditions dating back thousands of years, as Christian faith demonstrates. Or our values might be based on the culture surrounding us and what we think of as our own personal preferences. Or all the above.

Going to brunch on a Sunday morning with friends is a statement of value, just as attending a church service is too. The Bhagavad Gita and the *New Yorker* are very different documents, but people turn to both texts to understand and make meaning of the world around them. The level of authority those texts play in the life of any particular reader might vary dramatically. But both provide guidance in how to understand and move through the world around us.

At the same time, each of us establishes certain practices and relationships to experience or achieve more of the good we desire. Addictions step into that role of orienting our practices and relationships around that object of our desire.

Every person seeks to serve a "higher power," because every person is motivated to value something that is over and beyond themselves. We might not be fully aware that we are choosing a higher power, and our higher power may or may not be God. Our choices might be radically inconsistent with our values. But we all serve something or someone, whether we say we do or not.

Addiction is a form of worship. My hymn of praise to pain medicine, the poems of Coleridge, and the words of the relapsing woman on the street: these all reveal the ways that addiction closely resembles religious devotion. The popular form of medicinal opium in the Middle Ages up until the nineteenth century was called laudanum, from the Latin word *laudere*, meaning "to praise." And early enthusiasts did praise it.[7] Other common names included "the hand of God" or "the sacred anchor of life."

Writer David Foster Wallace, who explored addiction in depth in his novel *Infinite Jest*, warned a crowd of graduating college seniors at Kenyon College in 2005, "There is no such thing as not worshiping. Everybody worships." He warned of the dangers of worshiping power, money, or your own body, and then elaborated that the most dangerous thing about those objects of worship is that they reflect a cultural default setting. They are the things we can find our lives wholly aligned around and never even realize we made the choice to do so.

We define ourselves by the meaning that we pursue. Addiction is never just a journey for pleasure or entertainment, although it might look that way. It is always a journey of self-discovery gone wrong. It is a pursuit of a self that goes awry and destroys instead of expands who we are. It is worshiping at the altar of a substance or behavior that prom-ises freedom, safety, security, and certainty while eroding those very things.

Addiction exposes the uncomfortable reality that we are born into this world in pursuit of elusive knowledge, connec-tion, and meaning. Although we grasp for what is higher and beyond ourselves, there is still a danger, especially when we seek perfection.

18
Perfection

I have converted to Christianity—a lot. Growing up, I took almost every chance I was offered to raise my hand, walk down the aisle, fill out a form, or just say a small, quiet prayer in my heart.

My pattern was simple. I'd make a commitment to Christ, feel great excitement and moral purpose for one to two weeks . . . and then fall back into a life of adolescent sin. I'd determine that my prayer for salvation apparently hadn't worked, so I'd wait until the next opportunity, hoping that this time it would stick.

I had heard that faith was a race. I thought of my conversion as the starting gun to set me off down the road. Those first stretches I would approach with zeal and energy. But in no time, my breath would run short, I'd have a cramp in my stomach, and my legs would feel like lead. My lack of resilience, I believed, was because of some sort of failure in my start. The only option was to start it all again. One of these times, I figured, I'd start so well that I'd get straight through to the finish line without ever slowing down.

There were times when I wasn't sure if I should keep trying at all if I was going to keep screwing up and starting over. I figured there wasn't much point in moving forward until I knew how to do it right—until I could "be perfect," as Jesus had commanded. Indeed, Jesus hadn't made it easy. His words in a simple verse tucked away in the Sermon on the Mount have sent me into more than one bout of moral flagellation: "Be perfect, therefore, as your heavenly Father is perfect" (Matthew 5:48). There it is. The command is clear. The law is set. Be perfect; nothing less.

You don't need to be a Christian or even religious to feel this kind of pressure toward perfection. Cultural pressure and messages of attaining, and then maintaining, a kind of idealized life abound.

We now have the gift of instantaneous communication with large circles of friends and loved ones. Social media provides us a gift of connection with others, and it can burden us with an additional persona we must maintain and cultivate. We now need to be perfect for two: in the lives we live and the lives we project.

Those wrestling with and recovering from addiction find the pressure toward perfection to be strong. It is true, for some, that one slip-up can be devastating. Giving in to just "one drink" very well might not be just "one drink" but may instead set off a multiday binge.

Once a person has gained sobriety, the pressure to never falter again is real. Yet studies show that relapse is the standard, not the exception. Most people experience moments of return to a previous addiction.

But this tendency toward relapse—return to a behavior or way of being that we promised to forsake—is not unique to those who have been diagnosed with an addiction. It is, once again, part of all our lives.

May the one who has never relapsed cast the first stone.

Aspirations to a life of perfection—one free from all forms of relapse—is not just a harmful cultural narrative; it's a poor understanding of Christianity. Perfection isn't a goal; it's a temptation. Perfection is a pursuit of golden chains. The desire for perfection doesn't just impede recovery. Perfection can be an addiction itself.

Perfection run amok

In the early drive to cure addiction, doctors and chemists successfully moved opioid users from smoking or drinking opium to injecting morphine and then finally to injecting heroin. The intravenous injection, morphine, and heroin were all originally hailed as cures for addiction.

The idea driving this belief was that it was the "impurities" in opium that caused the addiction. If the substance could be refined down to only its beneficial, pain-relieving molecule, people thought, then whatever addictive properties were in the drug would be removed.

But this thinking—that the "good" anxiety-relieving molecules could be separate from the "bad" addictive ones—further fueled addiction. It failed to account for the fundamental reality that the "good" part of opium was one and the same with the "bad" part.

Ideas of perfection can also help fuel the addictive process. As we've seen, the same mechanisms and processes that go wrong within addiction overlap with what happens in anorexia or bulimia. Someone struggling with anorexia can experience a constant drive toward harmful behaviors but feel a sense of reward and accomplishment amid the self-harm. What may start as a small and controllable drive toward controlling what one eats can quickly become an obsession that someone can't stop thinking about.

My own story was not a straight line. I had three separate periods of relapse, each one around a new medical problem. The experience of intense pain, or in some cases a new surgery, triggered a desire for and usage of pain medicine that continued well after the immediate physical pain subsided. The temptation in each circumstance was to treat the relapse as I had my early conversion experiences. Recovery had been a sham, or at best a false start. If I hadn't made it all the way, why was I trying at all?

"Wholiness" versus perfection

"Progress, not perfection," is the old Alcoholics Anonymous maxim. It seems to stand in opposition with the biblical command to "be perfect."

But a closer look at the context of that command in the Sermon on the Mount shows a very different understanding. Biblical scholar Scot McKnight tackles the verse in his commentary on the Sermon on the Mount.[1] McKnight identifies the first part of the problem with what Jesus was actually saying and its connotations in the original language.

The Greek word used in the text, *teleios*, is often defined as "completion," "perfect," "mature," "adult," or "full development." In Greek philosophy, the term *telos* is used to describe something that fulfills its purpose in accordance with its identity. An acorn that grows into an oak tree would fulfill its telos.

We gain further insight when you consider that Jesus was probably speaking not Greek but Hebrew or Aramaic. The focus then becomes on words like *shalem* or *tamim*, which could be translated as "unblemished" and "whole."

McKnight runs through these possibilities and concludes that our modern idea of "perfection" isn't the best representation of what Jesus said. Instead, he writes, the term translated into our Bibles as "perfection" connotes "not the rigor of sinlessness but the rigor of utter devotion."[2] We need not so much to attain a standard as to commit to the pursuit.

But there is more to unearth. McKnight notes that the passage says not simply "be perfect" but "be perfect as your heavenly Father is perfect." Jesus is giving not just a general admonition but a particular moral weight to a character trait of the Father.

What is the focus? A few verses earlier, this section starts off with the familiar Sermon on the Mount refrain: "You have heard that it was said." In this section, Jesus tells his followers, "'You shall love your neighbor and hate your enemy.' But I say to you, Love your enemies and pray for those who persecute you" (Matthew 5:43-44).

Jesus does not demand that his followers throw on some light switch in their soul that leads to forever-sinless lives. Rather, he calls on a persecuted people, living under Roman occupation, to be utterly devoted to loving their enemies.

If you go back to the beginning of this famous sermon, you'll see that Jesus kicks it off with the Beatitudes. This is his famous list of those who are blessed, and includes the poor in spirit, those who mourn, the meek, those who hunger and thirst for righteousness, the merciful, the pure in heart, the peacemakers, the persecuted, and the reviled. The sermon is given in an explicit context of those whose lives are certainly not perfect. This list is immediately followed by a public rebuke of those who practice a kind of public piety or performative perfection.

In that sense, the Sermon on the Mount acknowledges the messiness of the world that we live in and that those who tend to most publicly espouse a kind of "perfection" are often the furthest from it.

Holiness can conjure up ideas of a life separated from the messiness, wants, needs, and passions of our daily human life. But holiness might be better understood as *whole*-i-ness. That is, we can think of holiness not as a state that we are either in or out of—holy or unholy—but as an ongoing pursuit of becoming whole. An utter devotion to progress, not perfection.

If we take seriously that sense of *telos*, then holiness isn't some idea of what perfection looks like that is handed down from religious leaders or culture. Instead, that encouragement to seek your telos—your purpose, your meaning—is as unique a pursuit as you are. The pursuit of my telos would mean not that I conform to a particular ideal but that I grow into the fullness of my unique identity.

One of the greatest dangers of perfection is that it fails to acknowledge that we see as through a glass darkly. We do not actually know what perfection is or what it looks like. Our limited and imperfect view of the world and ourselves means that all our projections of perfection are going to be distorted.

Our desire to know needs to be paired with a humility that we do not know. Our learning comes with an acknowledgment that we have unlearning to do. The ways we learn to see will continue to reveal how much we do not yet see.

Giving up on perfection isn't giving up on progress. It is the acknowledgment that we grow more in widening circles than we do in straight lines.

The idol and the icon

It is easy to make an idol of perfect recovery. Indeed, it is possible for anyone to make an idol out of a vision for any particular kind of life. The goal becomes attainment, not pursuit. When that happens, we lose the possibility of learning more about ourselves, the world, and what we are trying to attain.

Pursuit of perfection can become an addiction when we just keep doing the same thing over and over and expect a different result. When we set up standards we cannot possibly meet and then abandon our pursuit entirely out of frustration. This is the nature of idols.

An idol is never an idol without a worshiper. What changed the golden calf from a statue to an idol was the intention of the viewer. Jean-Luc Marion, in his work *God without Being*, notes that the same exact object can be either an idol or an icon, depending on the viewer.

An idol, Marion argues, captures the gaze of the viewer and keeps it affixed on itself. It "dazzles" the person with its

presence. But the captured gaze hides an
viewer from noticing that an idol is alwa
back to the viewer their own experience
and limitations. But all the idol is ever
reflection of the high-water mark of the viewer ,
ence with the divine.[3]

An idol convinces the viewer that they are glimpsing the
divine; in reality, it is showing the person a reflection of their
own self-perception and experiences. God, in this circumstance, becomes what Zorba the Greek described: "My god
is just like me, only bigger, wilder, and crazier!"[4] Or, as the
philosopher Ludwig Feuerbach accused all conceptions of the
divine to be, God becomes just a projection of human wants
and desires up into the clouds.

The icon, on the other hand, does not arrest the gaze of the
viewer. Instead, an icon invites the viewer to see past it, to the
realm of the divine. Whatever you see, you recognize that you
still don't see. Whatever you know, you recognize that you still
do not know.

Faith is simultaneously a journey and a waiting, a movement forward and a standing still. The turning around, the
stumbling, and the relapse; these are not signs that something is fundamentally wrong with you but evidence that you
have taken up the challenge and the invitation to try. You
have demonstrated the bravery of stepping out, not knowing
exactly where you are going but doing it anyway.

Life is not lived in pursuit of perfection but in creating a
wholeness large enough to hold the imperfection.

Widening circles

In the world of addiction and drug policy, the equivalent of this
understanding is called "harm reduction." The mantra of this
approach is "Any positive change." Harm reduction propo-
nents acknowledge that many people do not have a dramatic

...ion experience, in which addiction stops overnight. ...ad, it can require months or years of small steps toward ...sitive change.

Harm reduction is a public policy application of the theological idea that transformation begins when we "come as we are." As the LEAD program in Seattle demonstrates, sometimes the initial help creates the context for someone to give up their addiction.

Needle exchanges had been one of the more controversial applications of this approach, but their efficacy has now led to a wide-scale adoption of the program. Needle exchanges have been directly effective in stemming the spread of diseases like HIV, but they serve another benefit. At first, a person might come in just for a clean needle. But that is often a starting point for a relationship of caring trust. Those relationships can be a lifeline when the person who is using is ready to take the next step in their path to recovery.

The best public policy tends to be rooted in the belief that no one is perfect, no not one. But that doesn't mean we aren't deserving of help or another chance. This is "original sin" that doesn't alienate us from each other but binds us together in a common struggle. We can all admit that we don't grow in an uninterrupted line but, at best, in widening circles.

Rainer Maria Rilke wrote in his *Book of Hours*:

I live my life in widening circles
that reach out across the world.
I may not ever complete the last one
but I give myself to it.[5]

We are not stuck in a closed loop with no hope of improvement or movement. We can give ourselves to this outer circle even while understanding that we have not attained it. That utter devotion to what we haven't yet achieved becomes a source of strength that keeps us moving upward instead of a badge of shame that pushes us down.

Instead of looking down in shame because of our imperfections, we can look up in hope. To know our heavenly Father is perfect, in the way Jesus describes, is to know that we are not enemies of God. We are siblings to all creation and children of God, who extends the greatest love, boundless grace, and resounding mercy.

That goodness of God is large enough to hold us even while we are still in progress and incomplete.

19

Becoming

"What does being healthy again look like for you?" my doctor asked.

I hadn't reflected on this comment until I sat down to talk with Bill Miller, one of the world's leading addiction specialists. As soon as I told him about my doctor's question, he smiled knowingly. There was a lot more to the question my doctor asked me than I understood at the time. While I've never been able to confirm what was going through my doctor's head, chances are he said what he did because he was familiar with Miller's work.

Miller is friendly and unassuming. He looks like he belongs in New Mexico, where he makes his home. He is humble and soft-spoken about his accomplishments. I first spoke with him over the phone about a project unrelated to addiction. It took me a year to realize that the William R. Miller who kept coming up in my research was the same person as the Bill Miller I had spoken to on the phone.

For decades Miller has investigated how and why people change. His areas of study and research straddle two distinct fields: person-centered therapy and cognitive behavioral therapy. Person-centered therapy helps someone define who they want to be, what they want their life to look like, and how to get there. Cognitive behavioral therapy focuses on measurable outcomes and behavioral change. As opposed to exploring internal states of feeling or self-understanding, this school of thought examines and tests theories as to what ultimately causes and changes behavior; its well-known early origins are in the work of Pavlov.

With lessons from both fields, Miller founded a practice called motivational interviewing. It is a combination of the spirit and respect engendered within a person-centered therapy with the concrete, measurable, and actionable insight of cognitive behavioral therapy. The practice, he and his coauthor Stephen Rollnick write in *Motivational Interviewing*, "is about arranging conversations so that people talk themselves into change, based on their own values and interests."[1]

In motivational interviewing, the counselor or therapist is less the director of change than a witness to change. The method acknowledges that most people feel ambivalent about change: they simultaneously want things to be different but don't necessarily want to change their behaviors. Instead of trying to convince someone to change, motivational interviewing provides the context to help someone resolve their ambivalence and start a path to change.

My recovery did not start with naming what was wrong: my addiction to pain medicine. It began when I articulated what it would look like for me to be healthy again. Recovery began when I was able to describe my own values and desires, hopes and dreams, which would require being free from opioids.

That freedom wasn't just about not using the pain medicine anymore. It was also about being free from pain. The doctor who talked with me that day, my pancreatic specialist, could have called my primary care physician and the other doctors involved and let them know that he was cutting me off from pain medicine. That would have been the fastest way to pass along the problem of my addiction to another physician—as well as a surefire way to get me seeking alternatives.

Instead, we started with a vision for what a healthy life would look like. My doctor knew he needed to help me imagine health and well-being. He knew the best way forward was for us to work together to help my life and actions live up to those standards.

While motivation interviewing is not normally as dramatic as the moment between the prophet Nathan and King David, they both reflect a similar understanding of how people actually change. Transformation is found not in the imposition of an outside standard but in the cultivation of an internal one. The law, Paul would say, is already written on every heart (Romans 2:15). Our goal, and the key to effective treatment, is to call out something that already exists.

Confrontation

I had been "confronted" multiple times about my use of pain medicine. People have asked me many times now what made the final "confrontation" effective. The most important factor is a simple one.

My doctor's question wasn't a confrontation. At least not in the common sense of the word. It was, as best I can characterize it, a compassionate observation combined with supportive concern for my healing. Not very dramatic, but highly effective.

You might have seen in a television show or reality series an "intervention," in which a group of friends, colleagues, or loved ones, sometimes led by a professional, confront someone who is addicted with great dramatic affect. Interventions are designed to encourage the person experiencing addiction to admit they have a problem and seek help. Typically, those who have gathered share stories about the negative ways their lives have been affected by the person's addictive behavior. These interventions sometimes include ultimatums.

Miller links the origin of this practice to an understanding of addiction common in the mid-twentieth century. Lawrence Kolb, the original champion of the moral model of addiction, typified this attitude when he categorized "innocent" versus "vicious" addicts. Vicious addicts were considered moral degenerates who needed harsh confrontation and severe penalties if there was to be any hope of recovery.

Harry Tiebout expanded this thinking in his work with alcoholics, whom he deemed as having severe character problems and deep moral failings. Alcoholics propped up their addiction with defense mechanisms, Tiebout claimed, that could not be breached with typical therapy approaches. Instead, those with addictions needed to be "broken down" first before they could be "built up."

These beliefs were applied in a variety of ways. Some therapists adopted a harsh and combative tone with their patients; families brought in army sergeants or former convicts to get their kids "scared straight"; and some treatment facilities made new arrivals wear diapers and hold signs designating them "babies."

While the most extreme measures didn't make it into the mainstream culture, the idea of intervention as confrontation has.[2] A commonly held belief is that real addiction only turns around in one of two scenarios: either the person experiencing the addiction "hits rock bottom" or loved ones stage an intervention. "Rock bottom" always looks different, but it often involves losing a job, home, friends, or loved ones and possibly a run-in with the law. When a family is told that their only choice is to let their loved one "hit rock bottom" or stage an intervention, it's not surprising that some families choose the intervention.

The problem with interventions—and all forms of confrontational therapy, for that matter—is that they rarely work. In fact, there is good reason to believe that many of these approaches make things worse. Miller and his coauthor write, "Reviewing four decades of treatment outcome research, we found no persuasive evidence for a therapeutic effect of confrontational interventions with substance use disorders. . . . There is not and never has been a scientific evidence base for the use of confrontational therapies."[3]

It isn't just personal kinds of confrontation that are ineffective. One study evaluated a program designed to reduce drunk driving. Offending drivers were court-mandated to attend a seminar in which the victim of a drunk driver or a family member of the victim shares their story. When I first read about this program, I assumed it would serve as an effective deterrent against drunk driving. Far too often, we don't recognize the negative consequences of our actions until we put a face to the people we have hurt. Giving people more knowledge about the ways their actions can hurt others seemed like an obvious positive intervention.

But it isn't just information that matters; it is how you know that information. And for those who went through the program, the results were clear. Those who attended the seminar after their first drunk driving offense were *not* less likely to be rearrested for drunk driving than those who didn't attend the seminar. For those who had more than one offense and were mandated to attend, the rate of rearrest actually rose significantly.

Instead of calling people to be a better version of themselves, the program unintentionally reinforced people's worst perceptions of themselves. The information was accurate, but it came with a paralyzing shame. Why try to change when you believe you are a bad person? If you aren't "perfect," why try at all?

Empathy

Miller advocates for a fundamentally different stance toward people struggling with addiction. He understands therapy as a collaborative partnership in which the addicted person is always respected and maintains their own right to self-determination.

At the core of this person-centered approach is empathy. An empathetic counselor listens and reflects back to the patient what they are hearing. Empathy in this context isn't just a feeling but a specific skill that can be learned, practiced, and improved over time.

In one study, nine counselors were ranked on their level of skill in demonstrating empathy. Clients were randomly assigned to each counselor, and client outcomes were tracked over the course of two years. Even though each counselor had been trained in the same methodology and was using the same manual, they each had different results. The differences boiled down to one thing: empathy. The more empathetic the counselor, the greater the chance of the client's recovery. The less empathetic, the worse.

The evidence goes even further. In a multisite study conducted with thousands of participants, researchers compared various counseling approaches to help those struggling with addiction. For the methodology to be included, it already needed a body of evidence demonstrating its effectiveness.

This large study was designed to demonstrate once and for all which methodology was most successful in guiding addicts into recovery. When the results came in, the researchers were surprised: there was no significant difference between them.

What the study did show, however, is that each methodology's wide range of effectiveness *depended on the practitioner*. When researchers examined what might set the practitioners apart, what was the number one difference? The empathy rating the counselors received.[4] Subsequent studies suggest that most of the negative consequences come primarily from the least empathetic counselors. In fact, treatment with a non-empathetic counselor might be worse than no treatment at all.

Even if someone does not adopt the approach of motivational interviewing, Miller's work emphasizes how critical the approach of the counselor is. Recovery is never just about the theory behind the counseling but is always wrapped up in how the counselor approaches the relationship. A therapist can know what to say, but if that knowledge isn't embodied, it isn't effective. After a certain point, the methodology isn't as important as the empathy of the counselors themselves.

Empathy is important not just in a counseling relationship but for anyone who is working with those who are addicted. I talked with police officers, firefighters, and emergency department staff while working on this book, and a common theme emerged: they are tired and frustrated. They are on the front lines of the opioid crisis, and they have been asked to move a mountain with a pair of tweezers. It is little wonder that they sometimes curse the ground.

Support for people with addictions is just the start. We also need to support the people who work with those with addictions. Forward-thinking towns and counties are instituting therapeutic support for first responders to help them process the trauma they experience every day. Others are hiring specially trained staff to help address addiction in their communities directly.

Families of those addicted can easily and repeatedly experience burnout. A parent, sibling, cousin, or spouse might start off empathetic, only to feel burned time and time again. Frustration builds when a supportive loved one feels that they just can't help anymore. They feel taken advantage of if they give, and shame if they give up.

The importance of empathy does not mean that families and loved ones should never set boundaries. Boundaries don't need to be harsh treatment "for the good" of the person who is addicted. Boundaries are important because you need to make sure you still have love and empathy to give. If you give, or are taken advantage of, to the point where you resent the person struggling with addiction, it won't be good for either of you in the long run.

Despite my hesitance to describe that conversation with my doctor as a confrontation, Miller wants to redeem the word. He notes that the word *confrontation* means to bring "face-to-face." That, he argues, is exactly what people struggling with addiction need: to be brought face-to-face with their life, just as it is.

For Miller, confrontation is the *goal* of therapy, not a technique. The desire is to have patients come face-to-face with their lives and see a way forward past their own ambivalence and toward a path of change. Harsh confrontation might create a drama fit for television, but it fails all involved.

Trust in the slow work of God

Approaching addiction with empathy requires a kind of trust. It is the kind of trust Paul was referring to when he wrote, "I planted, Apollos watered, but God gave the growth" (1 Corinthians 3:6). It is not a guarantee that transformation happens overnight or even happens at all. We don't know what role we might play in helping another person toward recovery.

Empathy for ourselves and for others requires both time and space for growth. Pierre Teilhard de Chardin wrote:

Above all, trust in the slow work of God.
We are quite naturally impatient in everything
to reach the end without delay.
We should like to skip the intermediate stages.
We are impatient of being on the way to something
unknown, something new.
And yet it is the law of all progress
that it is made by passing through
some stages of instability—
and that it may take a very long time.[5]

This kind of trust requires us to slow down. Experience awe. Wake up to our own lives.

There is enough wonder in the world to heal us. You could write an entire novel about the stub of a mushroom lying on a cutting board, prepared for its journey into a meal. There is enough joy in the cooling presence of water that slakes our thirst to write a sonnet or even a ballet. To lose ourselves not in a barrage of attention-grabbing entertainment but in the fine-grain patterns of wood floors—in musing on the entire year of growth it took to produce just one line—leads to a kind of awe.

Contemporary life offers so many distractions and short-cuts. Promises of fulfillment to skip to the end without the struggle of the journey itself. Offers of the great vista without the work of the climb. Expectations of abundance without the labor of sowing and reaping.

This temptation to skip the wandering, to skip the in between, is not a new one. Wandering through the desert, the Israelites needed every inch of every mile of every path they trod. There is no shortcut to the promised land; if someone tells you there is one, you can know the land they are offering is a mirage.

This is not to say that there isn't a goal or a destination. There is. The journey is not the destination. But the journey is the place that transforms the wanderer so that the destination might truly be seen. You can show up at the right spot, the right place on the map, and not see the place for what it is.

We become dissatisfied with the journey and disdainful of the waiting. Moses was gone for forty days, and it wasn't long before the people demanded a god they could see. The story goes that Moses came down from the mountain, destroyed the words that God had given him, ground up the idol into the people's water, and then killed about three thousand of those who had been insufficiently faithful.

Our impatience can destroy us. Our demand for results now can poison us. The fastest is not always the best. The most expedient is not the greatest.

Addiction finds fertile soil in our dissatisfaction with the journey. Our desire is to skip through the hard places of becoming and settle into something that is complete. But we are not complete, and anything that offers that promise is an illusion. Some of those illusions are more dangerous than others.

Living a full life is, by necessity, a lifelong process. Fullness is only found in that cycle of being filled and emptied out, over and over again. Anything that promises more, faster, isn't real. Sometimes we are searching for the kinds of things that can only be found after a lifetime of work. Trying to skip ahead means we miss a whole lot and gain nothing.

Overcoming addiction is never found in the "do not." It is always found in the reorientation of your life and the giving over to the greater thing that you will do. A full life isn't found in the abstaining; it is found in the giving over of oneself to something greater that crowds out the addiction.

Nature abhors a vacuum, and so do our lives. Where we don't see meaning, meaning will come; it just might not be the meaning we are looking for. We must, as Teilhard de Chardin prays, learn to "accept the anxiety of feeling yourself in suspense and incomplete."[6]

20
Faith

In J. R. R. Tolkien's Middle Earth, we meet a small piece of jewelry that helps our hero, Bilbo, disappear. He uses it in times of need, and then he provides assistance to his friends in their times of crisis. Early danger signs are evident only in retrospect. The grip that the ring has on the hobbit only becomes clear when he is asked to give it up.

The ring shifts over time: from a tool that the wearer uses to a driving obsession. The ring's grip over Bilbo slowly grows, and shows its degenerative power in the sad character of Gollum. The story shows the depths of our divided hearts and the way that our aspirations for good can go terribly wrong.

I could go on and on about addiction and the ring in Middle Earth, but I recognize not everyone made their own capes and sat in maple trees reading Tolkien as children. Books, movies, and TV shows are full of these kinds of stories. Characters take in something seemingly innocuous, only to discover they did not understand what it was until it is too late. This mythology speaks to us in a rapidly changing world.

Seymour with Audrey II in *Little Shop of Horrors*, Dustin with Dart in *Stranger Things*, an entire unwitting population in *Gremlins*: all took into their homes something cute and innocent that soon grew dangerous and beyond their control. There are stories of children hiding pet alligators until the size, cost, and danger become clear. Pot-bellied pigs grow far larger than expected. Hagrid and his dragon Norbert, in the Harry Potter books, seem like a perfect match but ultimately cannot last.

In all these tales, our protagonists find themselves in situations they can no longer control. The initial choice they made was to take in something small and seemingly innocent. What they took in met a need. There was time of pure enjoyment while they were still in control. There was also a period of disbelief and denial: moments of clarity that things were going wrong, but stubborn insistence that a few small changes here and there would solve the problem.

Most people don't consciously make choices to bring chaos, confusion, hurt, or destruction into their lives. What can seem obvious in hindsight is not always clear to the decision-maker in the moment. The time that making different decisions would have been most effective is the time when the decision-maker has the least amount of reason or motivation to do anything differently. The heart is divided between a sense of affection and connection to something that used to give life when it morphs into something that drains life.

Some of these stories require the destruction of what was once beloved. Others require setting free or letting go. All of them require a moment of seeing: what was once believed to be under control is no longer.

All the relationships started with a sense of faith—a receptivity to an unexpected blessing. The plant, the little dragon, the cute small creature, the ring: these things had made some sort of promise or had a kind of promise projected onto them. The unwitting protagonists had a faith in that promise, even if it was unfounded. But the fact that it was unfounded simply undergirded the need for faith to try to actualize the promise.

So it was not just a faith, but a hope. A hope that things could be better, that the companion being nurtured would provide the connection or the protection the person had been longing for.

And in all these situations comes the complicating factor of love. It is a love that blinds the person to the growing destructive force at work in their lives. The early moments of help, comfort, and connection only serve to prolong the unhealthy relationship.

Addiction is a kind of faith gone wrong.

Journey of faith

Faith and addiction are both steps into things not yet fully known, and both are imbued with hope for a journey that will make things better. Both faith and addiction are defined by persistence in the face of negative consequences.

Addiction is misplaced faith, but it is a kind of faith nonetheless. The opposite of the addict is not the saint but the "lukewarm," Francis Seeburger writes. "The alcoholic or other addict stands in the shadow of the saint. In contrast, those who have never been addicted only because they lack enough passion for it are not even in sainthood's vicinity."[1]

Addiction offers a kind of organizing principle for life. As we discussed before, it relieves a burden of searching for a deeper meaning and provides an immediate—albeit shallow and unsustainable—answer.

Addictions represent finite answers to infinite longings. But adding up the finite over and over will never equal the infinite.

Faith, according to Hebrews 11, is "the assurance of things hoped for, the conviction of things not seen" (verse 1). There is always an element of not knowing within faith. Something remains beyond the grasp of the person who displays faith.

After listing myriad people who have demonstrated faith, the author of Hebrews writes, "All of these died in faith without having received the promises, but from a distance they saw and greeted them" (Hebrews 11:13). As with the idol and icon, there is both a knowing and a not knowing. A seeing and a not seeing. There is enough there to grasp, and still it is beyond our reach.

Faith, throughout this passage, is also marked by a persistence in a particular course of action, despite negative consequences. Faith means continuing to do the thing you feel compelled to do even if the initial joy and excitement is gone.

On the level of our brain activity, addiction is rooted in the natural processes of learning. On a spiritual level, I believe, addiction rises out of our capacity for faith.

Karl Clifton-Soderstrom, who argues that acedia is at the heart of the despair many feel today, also contends that the response to acedia is rooted in the virtue of faith. But faith, he explains, has traditionally been understood in the Christian tradition as a kind of gift from God. It isn't something we initiate but are given.

For a gift to become realized, it requires the action of the receiver. Faith and addiction are so closely linked because both depend on receiving something outside oneself—something that contains within it a promise of something good. Faith gone wrong can lead to addiction; then again, faith can help someone in the midst of addiction. "Faith is an activity characterized by receptivity and participation in the cycle of gift and gratitude," writes Clifton-Soderstrom.[2]

Faith is not controlled solely by the person exercising faith; rather, faith is a way of being that is open to and grateful for the gifts that come our way. Faith is characterized by a kind of stance we take in the world. Faith is a way of being more than it is a form of knowing.

"Bad faith," as we saw before, is a kind of self-deception that closes off the newness of possibility. Our focus narrows on the image of ourselves we are trying to preserve, and our receptivity to growth and transformation shuts down. We trade an illusion, which has often become comfortable, for the stretching challenge of faith.

When I imagine the origins of bad faith, I don't think of someone without faith at all. Instead, I imagine a faith that stagnated somewhere along the journey. As with the ring for Bilbo or a dragon for Hagrid, the person received the initial gift, and only later did it begin to destroy them.

The Hebrew people found manna every morning on the journey through the desert. They gathered it and ate what they needed for the day. But the moment they tried to hoard it and keep it, it would rot overnight. Thus, the gifts along the way must be discovered anew every day. They cannot be hoarded and saved or created in mass quantities and then sold.

This is how our ancestors lived. They celebrated the abundance when it was there, but then they prepared for the days, months, and seasons when it would not be there. Even amid absence, they lived with the understanding that the harvest would come again.

Instead of accepting manna—or blessing—when in season, we try to master it. We demand it again and again and again on our own terms and in our own time. What happened with the Israelites when they tried to keep this blessing on demand was that it rotted and was full of worms.

I fear that today our manna has rotted. But instead of seeing the worms, we've covered up the rot. We've learned to make it taste good. So the thing that is making us sick is the meal we continue to eat with abandon.

Gratitude

If faith requires a receptivity, then it is also connected to another virtue: gratitude.

I wish I had kept and framed the tinfoil cover of the small plastic container that held the first cranberry juice I sipped after weeks of being allowed nothing by mouth. The juice hit my tongue with the force of the first fresh strawberries of June after a spring of preparation. My mouth almost hurt with the burst of cool flavor. The lid's caveat—that the drink was no more than 10 percent real fruit juice—did not matter. It was the most grateful I ever remember being for just a few sips of liquid.

Periods of deprivation tend to do this. "Reward by an abundant good is largely determined by appetite," writes George Ainslie, an addiction researcher and behavioral economist.[3] We feel a greater sense of reward when we eat when we are hungry than when we are full. Hunger is a prerequisite to deep enjoyment of food.

It is little wonder I felt such gratitude when I could first drink again. I felt a sense of great reward for what was previously an experience I had taken for granted. I might not have enjoyed that tinfoil-covered cup at all under other circumstances. My sense of gratitude was connected with the higher level of reward I experienced because of the depth of my appetite.

We are built to become dissatisfied. This is not a generic moral statement but a physiological one. It is a description of how our sensory organs function.

The repeated stimulation of any of our senses leads to fatigue. This can be a good thing if you live on a farm and are spending a lot of time shoveling manure. Your sense of smell gets used to what is consistently present. It is also why we don't go crazy at the feeling of our clothes against our skin and why we are able to concentrate on the conversation of the person sitting across from us in a crowded restaurant despite five other conversations within listening distance.

As we've seen already, these are all adaptive ways that our brains help us focus on new information coming our way. In the case of that child learning to play T-ball, this dissatisfaction can become the positive desire to learn, grow, and develop new skills.

But for those of us who don't often experience much hunger or thirst, those rewards won't be very forthcoming. Cultivating a sense of gratitude isn't impossible, but it is challenging.

Gratitude interrupts our addictive tendencies. It acknowledges that a desire has been met. But instead of asking for more, a grateful person gives thanks for what has already been received. Gratitude can stop an addictive spiral before it starts.

The awe of seasons

Dopamine, as we've already seen, is released when the brain finds something about the environment that is better than expected. As soon as we begin to expect something, the dopamine release stops. When the dopamine dissipates, gratitude becomes more difficult. When gratitude fades, so does faith. Expectation destroys faith. But celebration can renew it.

I love my family's maple syrup tradition in part because it is one of the last widespread celebrations of an agricultural season. Across our region of New Hampshire, people boil in their own backyards or go to the nearest neighbor to gather inside a sugar shack or maple barn and celebrate the temporary abundance.

After my hospitalization, my brother was building up our family farm's production of maple syrup. We've since moved mostly to a tubing system to collect the sap, but that first year I was back home, we still had many of the old galvanized steel buckets hanging out on maple trees across the farm. The snow was deep that late winter and into early spring, and the collection process was slow.

Each bucket, at each stage, has its own special sound. First are the empty buckets and their muted *ting* of dripping sap falling straight to the bottom. Next is the *dop* that reverberates from the slightly sweet drop running off the spile to a thin layer of liquid below.

But it was the soft and all-too-rare *plop* that I waited for, with something akin to the anticipation of a child. That quiet *plop* (or sometimes *plip*) signals that the three-gallon bucket is over half full and that the tap is flowing in abundance. I would look at the tree and then its neighbors. I would slow and then strain to hear the rhythm of the buckets around me. And I would wonder for a moment about the generations who had harvested sap from these trees well over a hundred years before.

The teacher in Ecclesiastes writes famously, "For everything there is a season, and a time for every matter under heaven" (Ecclesiastes 3:1). This verse is often employed in both celebration and mourning to remind us of seasons of life. It is thought of as a kind of encouragement to cope with the changing season. But seasons are not just inevitable changes that we must endure; they are the very conditions that make life possible.

"Many today lack assurance that the inevitable demise of excitement will be followed by its rebirth in the fullness of time," writes Bruce Wilshire. "In fear of emptiness and inertness, ecstasy must be mechanically reinduced. Addiction is failure to trust the spontaneous recoveries of Nature and culture."[4]

We still know what seasons are, but we don't feel them the way our ancestors did. We are protected, by our technology, from the greatest ebbs and flows. Our success in transforming our environment comes with a loss of what it feels like to experience our environment. Our brains are wired to tune out the things that become familiar.

When I had a fentanyl patch on my arm, it kept the pain at bay. When I first took it off, what had become a relatively calm pool of numbed pain in my body and spirit formed waves again. These waves, the peaks and troughs of pain and relief, were not signs that my life had deteriorated; they were signs it was being renewed.

Joy does not make its home in things but jumps out into the space between them. Joy is found, discovered, and unwrapped. It finds its existence not as an object but as a gift always being given. It does not need to be dulled by repetition but can find its life most fully as it is practiced daily.

That joy, the reward, the satisfaction: these do not need to diminish with time if we learn to live with the seasons and cultivate gratitude over time. It is a kind of awe at wonder of the mundane and the regular.

Gratitude is wrapped up with faith, because being thankful for the gifts we have been given creates receptivity to the gifts that are yet to come. If newness, excitement, and gratitude define faith, it is little wonder that Jesus told his followers to "become like children" (Matthew 18:3).

Watching children, we are able to see a kind of wonder that many of us lose. We can see in them a level of gratitude for things that we have long since taken for granted. Those moments that shake us from the routine expectations of our lives are too few and far between. But it is often moments of awe and wonder that reset our sensory experiences and bring us back to gratitude.

Wilshire writes that it is not often that a person struggling with addiction is transformed "radiantly and at once." It often takes time and many setbacks. "But awe in the face of the universe and gratitude at being a small part of it—awe and gratitude that are not merely momentary—eat away at addictions."[5]

A good addiction counselor does not berate a patient who relapses but instead celebrates the length of time the person went without a drink or a hit. They encourage the person to be grateful for the progress they have made and to have faith that the strength they have shown can be demonstrated once again.

"Faith" as John Irving's Owen Meany says, "takes practice." It is a slow and steady way of opening ourselves up to the world around us. We no longer see through the tired and beleaguered eyes of an adult but with the new and fresh spirit of a child.

There is still mystery before us. There are still questions that remain unanswered. "Why is there any universe at all?"

Wilshire asks at the end of *Wild Hunger*. "Why not rather nothing? No answer is forthcoming, but that itself is a sort of answer. I know that nothing I can do will shed more light on the ultimate question. At crucial moments I need do nothing. Awe undermines addictions."[6]

Gratitude helps us rediscover the place where we began to hoard the manna we were given. In our thankfulness, we are able to be as children who can see the world as better than expected. It is not a sudden achievement at which we arrive all at once but is tied up with the humble anticipation of hope.

21

Hope

Every day I was in the hospital, I told myself I would be back home the next week. Then, when I was at home, recovering and hooked up to my pump, I was convinced that I'd be able to go back to work in just a couple of weeks.

My inability to deal with the reality of my predicament may have prolonged it. But these fantasies of a swift recovery were distortions of reality that I needed at that moment. And while I was practicing a kind of self-deception that avoided information too painful to grasp, I also held on to something else: good old-fashioned hope.

Two researchers, Leake and King, studied clients at three different alcohol recovery centers. After studying each person and analyzing their data, the researchers gave the staff some important feedback.[1] They told the staff which patients in recovery had the highest likelihood of staying sober.

When those who had been identified as likely to succeed were discharged, researchers tracked them. A year later, those individuals were still more likely than the rest to be employed and sober and to have had fewer and shorter relapses.

What had the researchers observed that allowed them to so accurately predict success? What characteristics or personality traits or work ethic distinguished those who stayed sober from those who didn't?

ually. The researchers homed in not on traits
:s themselves but on the expectations of the
very clinics. They told the counselors and staff
was more likely to recover than the other. They
didn't say this to the people in recovery; just to the staff.

In other words, *the expectations of the staff changed the outcome for those in recovery.* The staff's belief that someone would recover helped create the conditions in which that person could recover. A belief in someone else's recovery became a self-fulfilling prophecy of the best kind.

What we think about addiction is shaped by what we think about those who are addicted. And what we think about those who are addicted can dramatically change the outcomes in a person's life.

"Hope is a powerful healer," remarks Miller.[2] That isn't just a nice sentiment. Hope is not just an esoteric inspiration but a force that can create a physiological change. Our ability to envision a better future can change the chemicals in our brains and the connections of our neurons. One study showed that those who consistently took a placebo as a treatment for alcoholism had better outcomes than those who didn't.[3] It didn't matter what was in the pill; recovery was in the act of doing something that you believe can make a difference. In AA, a common saying is "It works if you work it."

This is true of the hope we have for ourselves, but as this study demonstrates, it is also true of the hope we have for others. The hope that we hold for those in our lives can help bring about the change we believe is possible.

The opposite is true as well. Subsequent studies demonstrated that the change in effect largely had to do with changing the views of a small group of negative counselors. As we saw before, the more negative confrontation a counselor uses, the worse the outcomes for the client. In fact, a counselor with a negative attitude produces worse results than no counseling intervention at all. Just the tone of voice a doctor uses when talking about those struggling with alcoholism is predictive of whether that person will stay in a recovery program.[4]

Imagination

Imagination both fuels our desires and changes them. We read a story, watch a movie, or hear a speech by an inspirational person and we walk away ready to take on a new goal or tackle an old challenge.

One of my most productive writing times while working on this book was after seeing a documentary about Ruth Bader Ginsburg. Something about watching the eighty-something Supreme Court justice go to the gym and hold a plank for sixty seconds while fighting in court for the rights of the oppressed—well, it made me want to get up at five in the morning and keep writing.

Through imagination, our desires, impulses, and instincts can become filled with meaning. In our imaginations we picture the person we could be if we were to pursue our desires or adopt new ones. Imagination is an essential part of who we are. This is the space that allows us to move past our present moment and imagine a future full of possibility. We are able to see beyond what is in front of us to all that could be. And the strongest moments of our imagining are the ones for which we have hope that they can actually come to pass.

Our imagination isn't just "all in our head"; what occupies our imaginations is indelibly connected to our bodies and how they function. If a little bit of salt water that I pushed into my veins had the power to release chemicals that ease pain and anxiety, imagine what encounters with hope can do to our brains.

Imagination is a force for healing in our own lives and within our society. Theologian Walter Brueggemann lifts up the incredible power of what he calls "the prophetic imagination."

This kind of imagination projects new possibilities into the world, with the understanding that we cannot create a better world if we cannot first see it with our imaginations. "The prophet engages in futuring fantasy," writes Brueggemann. "The prophet does not ask if the vision can be implemented, for questions of implementation are of no consequence until the vision can be imagined. The imagination must come before the implementation."[5]

Cultural change begins with imagination. We need to see a new and better way of living with each other before we can start to build that culture. A culture in which the status quo is the only possibility narrows our vision to nothing more than a maintenance of basic needs, distractions, and petty pleasures.

Brueggemann warns, "Our culture is competent to implement almost anything and to imagine almost nothing."[6] The technocratic skill and capacity we have developed has not translated into fulfillment and happiness. Sisyphus might find faster ways to roll the stone up the hill, but it doesn't give the work purpose and meaning. With a prophetic imagination, Sisyphus might ask if it is time to abandon his stone altogether.

Jesus talked about the kingdom of God as being both here and not yet. Just because it isn't here doesn't mean it isn't real. Those who have "eyes to see" a new way of living and being in the world are transformed by the sight itself (cf. Matthew 13:16). As we begin to imagine what God's kingdom is like, there is a sense in which it begins to exist among us. The more we can envision the way things could be, the more we have the capacity to act as if they already are that way.

Howard Thurman, a contemplative teacher and Civil Rights leader, wrote of this imagination as dreams in his book *Meditations of the Heart*. "The dream is the quiet persistence in the heart that enables a man to ride out the storms of his churning experiences." He continues, "It is the exciting whisper moving through the aisles of his spirit answering the monotony of limitless days of dull routine. It is the ever-recurring melody in the midst of the broken harmony and harsh discords of human conflict."[7]

I'm not saying we can daydream our way into a better world. I am saying that if we can't even dream a better world, than we certainly won't be able to make one.

Incarcerated hope

If hope is necessary for recovery, then the worst thing we could do to those struggling with addiction is remove hope from their lives—which is exactly what we do in the criminal justice system today. The ongoing War on Drugs and system of mass incarceration in the United States are not only an ineffective waste of money; they actively contribute to the destruction that drugs can cause.

Those living in recovery need to be able to imagine what that new life looks like and to maintain the hope that they can achieve it. Addiction diminishes our capacity to weigh the long-term pros and cons of our behavior—something that we as humans are pretty bad at already, even without the added complication of an addiction.

For those struggling with self-harming behavior in the present, increasing punishment in the future doesn't help them improve their behavior. Punitive criminal punishment without comprehensive support for recovery makes the situation worse.

A lot worse.

A study of more than 1,300 injecting drug users in Baltimore from 1988 to 2000 examined this problem. Researchers examined demographic factors, drug use patterns, and even whether the person sought drug treatment. The authors write, "Of great interest is that only a history of incarceration differentiated persons who successfully stopped using drugs from those who continued to use injection drugs over a 12-year period." This bears repeating. The only factor that distinguished those who successfully stopped using drugs from those who continued to use was this: those who stopped had not gone to prison.[8]

A fifteen-year study of 100,000 "juvenile offenders" found that those who were sentenced to some sort of incarceration were three times more likely to be incarcerated again as an adult than those who had the charges dropped or participated in an alternative sentencing program.[9] The researchers note that the effects are strongest for those who are incarcerated between the ages of fifteen and seventeen, when the punishment is most likely to interfere with finishing high school.

Kids who lose hope for a better future are never going to do as well as those who can keep hope alive. It is a lot easier to keep hope alive when we give people a good reason to.

When looking across the globe in a study for the UK government, researchers found no direct correlation between the punitive punishment a country had for using drugs and the rate at which people are using them.[10]

Portugal, in 2001, became the first and only country in the world that has gone to the extreme of decriminalizing all drugs for personal use. Drugs aren't legal, but if someone is caught with a small amount, there are only civil fines to be paid. Money that had been used for incarceration and the criminal justice system has been reallocated to outreach and treatment programs.

At the time of the law change, approximately 1 percent of the population was regularly injecting heroin. Even today in the United States, the percentage is just under 0.5 percent. Critics across the world warned that a huge spike in both usage and overdoses would soon follow. But in 2017, Portugal had one of the lowest drug overdose rates in the European Union, at 6 per million inhabitants compared to 21.3 per million for the European Union at large. In the same year, Portugal's population of all "high-risk" users of opioids, including IV heroin, was under 0.5 percent.[11]

When I first saw these numbers, I was intrigued, because I had just read that our overdose rate in the United States was 21.7—close to the European Union as a whole but still nothing close to what Portugal had achieved. When I went back to check the numbers again, I noticed my mistake.

In the United States, we count drug overdoses per one hundred thousand, not per million. The comparable numbers are 6 per million in Portugal, 21.3 per million for the European Union, and 217 per million in the United States.[12]

This is not to say that decriminalization is a panacea. The overdose rate in Portugal has risen in recent years. And while the number of people who report having used drugs in the past twelve months has gone down, the number of people reporting use of any drug has gone up.

The architect of the change in policy, Dr. João Goulão, is concerned that some might take the wrong lessons from what has happened in Portugal. "It's very difficult to identify a causal link between decriminalization by itself and the positive tendencies we've seen," he said. "It's a total package. The biggest effect has been to allow the stigma of drug addiction to fall, to let people speak clearly and to pursue professional help without fear."[13]

The key is not decriminalization per se but holding a place for hope for anyone wrestling with addiction. Over half of all resources dedicated to drug policy in Portugal go toward "demand reduction," which is treatment, not incarceration. Portugal is a unique country with a particular history. What works there will not necessarily work here. But it does show that harsh criminal penalties are part of the problem, not the answer.

Prayers of hope

For years I was suspicious of prayer. Before I was suspicious, I just felt bad at it. My early prayers as a child included long lists of "Please bless . . ." and, my parents report, a nightly request to God that I would not have any dreams about princesses. (I'm not sure I want to know what Freud would have to say about that one.)

But as a young adult, I realized that my conception of prayer didn't make a lot of sense. Up until that time, I had thought about prayer as a fairly unreliable magical incantation. So as a young person, I abandoned it. I didn't consciously jettison prayer altogether, but I functionally left it along the roadside of childhood and teenage belief. If I wasn't sure of prayer's purpose, why would I do it?

Prayer, I knew, was a spiritual practice. For years, I interpreted the word *practice* as "requirement." Spiritual practices were just another long list of things I was supposed to do. It took me a long time to see them as actual practice for a good and flourishing life.

Prayer is a practice that mediates between the conscious self and the automatic self. Meditation and mindfulness, close cousins of prayer, have now emerged at the heart of many recovery methods. Prayer and meditation are very literal "practice" for being a different way in the world. They are methods of beginning to live out and create what we hold in our prophetic imaginations.

I don't believe that prayer is simply a means to an end. There is a good inherent in the practice. But for me, I began a journey back to prayer and meditation because I began to see the practical benefits in my life.

I don't just pray because I am hopeful; I pray to become hopeful. I pray in order to imagine a different way the world and my life can be. I pray in order to slowly help change myself into the kind of person who can help make that better world more realized every day.

Richard Rohr notes in *Breathing Under Water* that the most universal addiction is "our own habitual way of doing anything, our own defenses, and most especially, our patterned way of thinking, or how we process our reality."[14] This is true of my own life. I get in a loop in my head that I can never seem to exit. I rehearse the wrongs that I feel were done to me, and I come up with clever and biting responses (at least, they are clever and biting in my head).

One of my entry points to understanding the significance of prayer in the midst of addiction was Jesus' words to his followers in the Sermon on the Mount to "love your enemies and pray for those who persecute you" (Matthew 5:44). Coming into adulthood soon after 9/11, I thought of Osama bin Laden and the Taliban as enemies. But as I got older, I began to think of my enemies as any person, or situation, that got me into one of those obsessive loops in my head about response and revenge.

So what does it mean to pray for the person who is the object of my anger? Luke records his version of Jesus' saying to include "do good to those who hate you, bless those who curse you, pray for those who abuse you" (Luke 6:27-28). Prayer helps me reframe situations. Instead of looking to blame the other and to exact the kind of revenge I am looking for, I begin to think about what it means to do good and bless in response. Prayer becomes an interruption of the neural loop. It begins to activate and engage other parts of my brain.

Sometimes I'm even able to hold that person in compassion. As I think about what a blessing for them might look like, I can begin to imagine, from their perspective, what might have brought us to this situation. Why might they have done what they did? Was there a hurt or a wrong in their life that they were responding to? Were they actually aiming at something good and important when they missed the mark and hurt me? And in praying for good and blessings in that person's life, how can I be the answer to that prayer?

If it is true that what "wires together fires together," then that means the longer I stay with my downward spiral of negative thinking about someone else, the more likely I am to slip into those negative patterns the next time I interact with that person—or in the case of being angry at a stranger, the more likely I am to act defensive the next time I'm around a stranger.

My pain counselor gave me a book on meditation and pain. She had told me to stop resisting the pain and get to know it and understand where it was coming from. Later, I'd learn from Cynthia Bourgeault, a contemplative teacher, that meditation and prayer are less like a computer program you choose to run and more like a transition to an entirely new operating system. This operating system would change not just a part of who I was but my whole way of functioning.

I'm still not sure what I believe about how prayer changes things. That remains mysterious for me. But I do know that I am changed by prayer. Through prayer, God shapes my imagination and desires in ways that can shift and change how I act in the world.

In addiction, the "enemy" isn't just outside yourself, but inside you. The hope is not in defeating the enemy but in transforming the enemy into a friend through love.

22

Love

There is a legend that after Jesus ascended to heaven, Martha, along with her sister Mary and brother Lazarus, boarded a ship without sails, oars, or a rudder. The ship brought them from the coast near Jerusalem to Marseilles in what is now France.

There, on a rock in the river Rhône, a great dragon sat, having come across the sea from Galicia. Its wings protected it on either side like armor, and it was as strong as twelve lions or bears. With one snort of fire, it could turn an entire acre of woods to glass. Named Tarasconus, the dragon lurked there in the river, destroying every ship that passed and killing everyone who tried to stop the beast.

But when Saint Martha discovered Tarasconus eating a man, she set out to tame the dragon. Where all the battles with swords, spears, arrows, and catapults had failed, Saint Martha, armed only with holy water and a cross, succeeded in making Tarasconus as still as a sheep. So docile was the dragon that she bound him only with a sash from around her waist.

Dragons, in most mythologies, are defeated by physical force and the strength of a knight's will. The hoarding beasts are overcome only through violence. But dragons are also a symbol of our interior struggles; they are reflections of the worst aspects of ourselves. They collect gold and riches but do not enjoy them; they do not have companions but capture women out of their insatiable desire for dominance. They are a projection of unbridled human desire for more.

It is "the very nature of addiction to feed on our attempts to master it," writes Gerald May.[1] Addiction is a dragon that is overcome not through battle but through a kind of taming and redirection. Our addictions, no matter how they started, are a part of us. They began at some point out of a desire for some sort of good.

If we threaten that part of ourselves with death, it will do whatever it can to survive and fight back.

Willpower will not save you

It would be easy to imagine victory over addiction as the dominance of willpower over the dragon of "the flesh." But our willpower isn't a sword or a mighty weapon.

When we talk about willpower, we usually mean our capacity to feel competing desires and choose the "better" option. The "better" part is often what we have consciously chosen versus impulses or desires that come from the automatic self. Willpower, then, is often a conscious disruption of an otherwise automatic process.

One popular view of willpower is that it is like a muscle: you can strengthen it over time, but it is limited in supply and can be drained quickly. To imagine how quickly it gets worn down, think of the videos you may have seen of adorable children sitting in front of a marshmallow that has been placed there by a researcher. The researcher promises the child a second marshmallow if the child refrains from eating the tasty treat until the researcher comes back with another one.

We watch as the children physically express what many of us feel inside when trying to resist temptation. They wiggle and squirm, hold themselves back, distract themselves, look away, nibble, and then maybe they lick. Many of them give up and just eat it. The hope is that if children can learn how to exercise self-control in relation to the marshmallow, they'll have the willpower they need to be successful in other areas of life.

But if willpower is like a muscle, it seems to be a highly specific one. A professional athlete requires a great deal of self-control and discipline in exercise and practice, but that doesn't always translate into self-control in spending habits. A high-powered attorney might exercise great financial restraint in running a firm—until it is destroyed by the attorney's unrestrained alcohol and pill consumption. William Wilberforce demonstrated remarkable dedication in his quest to end the slave trade in Great Britain, but he was unable to quit his opium addiction.

"For the addicted person alone, struggling only with willpower, the desire to continue the addiction will win," Gerald May writes. "Willpower and resolutions come and go, but the addictive process never sleeps."[2]

Ultimately, the concept of willpower in recovery fails because it treats the automatic self as an enemy to be conquered. The conscious self becomes the knight in shining armor, wielding willpower as a weapon to slay the dragon of addiction. Addiction is hard to overcome because it does not reside primarily in the conscious self. The grooves, the pathways in the snow, have been carved deeply in automatic processes—so deeply that they have changed the very way that our brain looks and responds to basic stimulus.

The image of Martha and the dragon gives us a rubric for approaching recovery. If we understand that our addictions are always rooted in some desire for good, we can see that the dragon is not a personification of "pure evil" but a projection of the destructive nature of our own misdirected desires.

As we've seen, there is no "addiction center" in the brain that can or should be destroyed. While dopamine is a chemical that makes addiction possible, it is a chemical we wouldn't do well without either.

At the end of the legend, in images depicted in many works of sacred art, Saint Martha binds the dragon with only a piece of cloth. If you are going to imagine willpower being a part of the story, think about it as being just about as strong as Martha's sash.

Overcoming addiction requires us not to fight the dragon but to tame it. The best ways to control our selves is not always to rely on what we normally think of as self-control. Prayer and meditation are tools that can bring us to that place of calling an enemy a friend. The formation of new habits and strategies for changing our behavior learned through counseling like motivational interview or cognitive behavioral therapy can help produce long-term change. What we once battled we have now enlisted as an ally. What we once feared has now been transformed by love.

Agape

Maybe you've noticed something about this book. I spend a lot of time returning to that one conversation with one doctor. There are certainly a lot more stories to tell.

I didn't set out to focus so much on one moment. But while I was writing, I was drawn time and time again to that one encounter. It was, in the best sense of the word, a profound "confrontation." I didn't understand my own preoccupation with this one conversation until I read about a mystery that Dr. Bill Miller set out to solve.

In the world of therapy, length or amount of treatment is often correlated with better outcomes. But early in Miller's research, he found what he thought was an anomaly. He compared outcomes for those struggling with alcoholism who received five hours of counseling versus those who received twenty-five hours of counseling. After twelve months, both groups improved at roughly the same rate.

Next, he compared outcomes for those enrolled in a ten-week self-control outpatient program with those given a single session of encouragement and a self-help guidebook. Both groups showed a reduction in drinking, and there still wasn't a significant difference between the two. When he couldn't believe the results, he repeated the study twice. This time, he included not just a ten-week program but an eighteen-week program. The other group still received just one session and a book. Once again, everyone made progress, and there were minimal differences between all the groups.

One possible explanation, Miller thought, is that the real effect comes from the fact that everyone who participates in any of these trials wants to change. You wouldn't sign up for any program unless you wanted something different for your life. In his next round of studies, Miller created another control group of people who were on a wait list for the study versus those who had gotten in to the study. That way, he could know that everyone wanted to change but only certain groups would receive the interventions he was testing.

Once again, there was little difference between the group that received an encouragement session and a self-help book and the group that received longer and more intensive therapies. But the people on the wait list experienced no improvement while they were on the wait list. As soon as the researchers repeated the study and the wait list group was accepted, Miller saw the same across-the-board patterns as before.

Miller began to look around and discover that other researchers had similar findings. Brief but empathetic sessions with a counselor could have a surprising impact. In one study, individuals who were admitted to the ER for alcohol-related problems either were treated as usual or received usual treatment *plus* a brief empathetic intervention. Those who received the empathetic intervention were ten times more likely to seek help for their alcohol problems than those who didn't have the conversation. When it came to those who stuck with it, the effect was even larger.

Miller asks, "What might frame the substantial observed effects of these interpersonal interactions? What do we know that (a) is interpersonal, (b) even in . . . relatively small doses can have a marked and sometimes profound effect, (c) seems to work by decreasing negativity, and (d) the more severe the problem, the larger the response?"[3]

The only thing he could imagine that would be so powerful is love. Not just any kind of love, but agape love. Agape is the highest form of love that encompasses everyone and everything (John 3:16). In medical ethics, Miller and his coauthor note, it is called beneficence. In Buddhism it is *metta*, in Judaism it is *hesed*, and in Islam, *rahmah*.[4]

In light of what Miller has found, the significant meaning I place on that one conversation shouldn't be surprising. The moment of nonjudgmental acceptance I experienced at a time when I was receptive and needed it was a turning point. For those like me who are lucky enough to have a compassionate encounter with a counselor at a moment of need, these brief interventions can be life-altering.

The presence of love as a part of my healing does not mean that love had been absent before. As you've read my story, you've seen that I was surrounded by people who loved and cared about me. Love doesn't mean that we will be immune to addiction.

Part of what made the encounter with that doctor a powerful and memorable one was its unexpected nature. Something in that moment made my entire being shake awake and say, "Pay attention! Something happening here is better than you anticipated." There are a lot of factors that led to that being a moment when I was receptive to not just hearing but beginning to embody new information.

The story of Jean Valjean in *Les Misérables* is often held up as an example of the transformative power of an unexpected gesture of grace and love. Valjean was not transformed when he was offered a meal and a bed for the night. He did not change when the bishop told the police that the goods Valjean was carrying were not stolen but were gifts. It wasn't until Valjean witnessed himself steal from a small boy that the contrast of the love he had been shown and the reality of his own actions changed him.

This research does not denigrate the importance of therapy in the road to recovery. It lifts up the outsized effect small acts of love, compassion, and empathy can have in the lives of those struggling with addiction.

Miller finishes his recounting of this research with the words of Teilhard de Chardin, "The day will come when, after harnessing [space], the winds, gravitation, we shall harness for God the energies of love. And, on that day, for the second time in the history of the world, [we] will have discovered fire."[5]

Just say yes

Love gives us something to say yes to. Blame is only about a *no*.

Overcoming addiction is never accomplished in negation. Recovery is not ultimately about the things we don't do, or the substances we don't take, or the people we stay away from. Rather, recovery comes in the positive commitments we make that can replace the addiction. Every addiction has some sort of good at which it is aimed. If we remove the addiction but don't give ourselves a new way to achieve that good, then we are bound to fail.

Jesus tells his followers that when an unclean spirit has gone out from a person, it wanders around trying to find a new home. When it doesn't find one, it says, "'I will return to my house from which I came.' When it comes, it finds it empty, swept, and put in order. Then it goes and brings along seven other spirits more evil than itself, and they enter and live there; and the last state of that person is worse than the first" (Matthew 12:44-45).

Equating addiction with demon possession is dangerous, of course. It can overspiritualize the problem, as if it comes from outside a person and not from inside ourselves. But you can imagine that for people living at the time of Christ, a demon was probably the best language available to describe something like addiction. To watch others struggle with addiction can look as if a foreign invading force has taken over their actions. I've felt that sensation of watching myself continue down a path while stuck inside my head alone with my vain protests.

If we try to make recovery solely about self-denial—stopping the use of a drug or changing a behavior—we leave an empty house. If we try to make it about our exercise of willpower to keep the door closed, when the seven demons come knocking, we will fail.

Once someone quits, there can be a lot of time to fill. One of the reasons AA can be so helpful for those in recovery or seeking sobriety is a very simple one. Going to a meeting is something to do that isn't your addiction. The more severe an addiction is, the more activities and actions of life revolve around that addiction, the more addiction becomes your foundation. In those cases, it can require a substantial building project to create a new life that isn't built on shifting sand.

Recovery meetings can be beneficial as a place to hear wisdom from others who have had similar experiences. You can take advantage of accumulated knowledge about recovery. Meetings provide connection with people who can support you in your journey. And new habits are always best when formed in a community where people are all practicing in similar ways together.

One neurobiologist—addiction researcher and recovering alcoholic Owen Flanagan—is critical of some aspects of AA. In fact, court-mandated AA has been shown to be ineffective and even harmful. But for those who go voluntarily and invest in it deeply, there can be significant benefits. That is why when it comes to his own recovery, Flanagan still goes. Even his philosophical and scientific critiques do not outweigh, for him, the practical benefits of being part of such a community.[6]

The interpersonal experiences of love and unconditional acceptance combined with the habits and practice that AA provide are all a part of transformation. Love is present in community, not isolation.

For those who love someone struggling with an addiction, I hope this is an encouragement. There is a temptation to try to shoulder all the burdens of another's struggle, but that is not possible. The kind of love that creates a context for healing always comes from a community. There are lots of roles to play. No one person can be everything to another person in recovery.

The temptation to keep on sacrificing for another is real. But sacrifice is not the same as love, and sacrifice does not always indicate the presence of love. The prophet Hosea, delivering a message from God says, "I desire steadfast love and not sacrifice" (Hosea 6:6). If a friend or loved one is wrestling with an addiction, there is a danger you could turn yourself into a scapegoat. You could fall into a trap of requiring a sacrifice of yourself as absolution. Sacrifice is saying no; love is saying yes to something greater.

The challenge of what we will say yes to is there in each of our struggles to address addictions in our own lives. But the challenge is also there for communities and countries: What does it look like to say yes to a culture of healing?

Compassionate curiosity

A love for yourself does not preclude a desire for change; it often precedes it.

One practice recommended by some addiction counselors is compassionate curiosity. The primary stance we need to take with ourselves is not one of a judge meting out a sentence. When we approach ourselves in a manner of condemnation, we normally try to justify ourselves and our behavior. Justification brings us to a place of vigorously defending whatever we just did. We shift blame away from ourselves to external sources and explanations.

We might even make a lot of good points. Our life might be particularly stressful; the person at work might indeed be very annoying; a spouse or loved one might actually be acting selfishly. All these things might be cause for drinking more than we should, eating more than we need, lashing out in ways that will cause harm, or even just watching hours of thoughtless television.

Our thoughts can run on a self-reinforcing loop. When we first start thinking about our actions, especially problematic ones, we feel ambivalent. Some of our thoughts focus on reasons we might sustain the behavior, while others orient around reasons to change. If we feel threatened and defensive, all it takes is a few minutes of justification to entrench the bad behavior or to remain in ambivalence indefinitely. We may even move from excusing our behavior to believing we have chosen the only possible course of action—maybe even a righteous one.

Self-justification is only a hair's breadth away from self-deception. The justification is not just outward but also inward. We justify our choice to take the pill or eat the whole bag of chips because we believe we are not capable of doing otherwise. *Of course* that is the way I acted, we might think; I am nothing more than an addict. Things could not have gone otherwise, because I am bad, weak, or deficient.

Compassionate curiosity is different from self-justification or self-blame in that it seeks first to *understand*, not judge. Compassionate curiosity can explore the circumstances or factors that led to the behavior. Self-justification says, "Of course that happened again; [fill in the blank] drove me to it!" Self-blame says, "Of course I relapsed; I'm too weak not to!" Compassionate curiosity, however, prompts us to gently ask ourselves, "I wonder why I just did that again?"

Ultimately, we need to look not only at specific actions but at the kind of person we are and are becoming. Compassionate curiosity helps us focus on our best desires and intentions and allows us to see where they went wrong and how we went off track.

When we assume the best about ourselves, we are better able to do the same for others. We fully love our neighbor when we are able to love our neighbor *as ourselves*. In the process of finding the best of our intentions, we don't ignore the ways we've gone wrong but instead draw our imagination to a life lived in line with the best of our own values and commitments.

Part of why love is so effective in addressing addictions might be because of how much love resembles addiction. Neuroscientists have found that brain scans of someone in the early stages of romantic love and someone addicted to drugs look remarkably similar. Both addiction and love are able to orient a person with a laser focus on achieving a goal. One sign of addiction is when the person uses the drug for much longer periods than intended. They "lose time" in the same way people do when they are with someone they love.

While the similarities are striking, over time the two phenomena diverge. One research paper describes it this way: "Although romantic love and drug addiction are similar in the early stages, they are different in subsequent stages, as the addictive characteristics of love gradually disappear as the romantic relationship progresses. However, the addictive characteristics are gradually magnified with repeated use of drugs of abuse."[7]

An intense romantic love has the capacity to develop into a healthy, stable, long-term relationship. Learning to love your partner increases your capacity for other kinds of prosocial behaviors. Addiction, on the other hand, creates dysfunction. In the first case, you get an increased capacity for being your best kind of self. In the second, you increasingly lose control over consciously deciding who you are and what you want to do.

Addiction fuels a desire that can never be quenched, while love increases a connection that has no end.

23

Grace

Recovery is always a miracle. It is a miracle not because it requires special dispensation from God or because someone curries unique favor with the gods. Recovery is a miracle because life is a miracle.

During one of my hospital stays, my brother, who was teaching high school in Chicago, spent a week of his winter break with me. He stayed at my apartment and walked to the hospital each day to spend time with me. We watched the Indiana Jones movies together, laughing at how our grandmother had taped *Raiders of the Lost Ark* from television so we could fast-forward through the commercials and any scenes she deemed inappropriate. (It was years until I saw the scene of melting Nazis at a normal speed, and I am here to say it is far more traumatizing to watch in fast-forward.)

We talked about my brother's fiancée, and about his upcoming wedding. He invited me to be his best man and gave me updates on Peder, a friend he had invited to be one of his groomsmen. Peder had been my brother's housemate in college and then again the year after they graduated.

Peder had a rare form of liver cancer, and the week my brother was with me, he would call Peder in a hospital in Chicago and put me on the phone. Peder and I would commiserate about hospital stays, and the tests and scans we'd get woken up for in the middle of the night. I told him if I got out of the hospital first, I'd come visit him.

Months later I booked my flight to go see him. I was still sick and maybe not well enough to travel, but I wanted to try anyway, because I learned Peder had been moved into hospice care.

The trip never happened. One day before my flight, Peder died.

Was this the world of punishment and reward? Had God somehow seen fit for me to live and for Peder to die? Or had Peder simply drawn the short straw? Had I been more righteous? Had his parents sinned? Had he sinned? Had I gotten better doctors? Did God decide that we could all learn a lesson by watching a twenty-three-year-old die—a lesson better learned than if a twenty-five-year-old had died? Was there a grand cosmic plan that continued on for me but was over for him?

Most of the time, I try not to think about the faces behind the nearly two hundred people who die of drug overdoses in the United States each day. The father who finds his son with a needle in his arm. The mother whose voice shakes at a school board meeting when she speaks up about her daughter's true cause of death. The woman who is facing withdrawal alone and wondering if it is worth going through all the pain because she isn't sure there is anyone left who loves her. The man who walks out of prison unsure whether his life is worth going back to and wondering if his best hope for a job is with his old dealer.

What is the grand design at work? The truth or lessons we could somehow not otherwise learn except through all this suffering?

I understand that God's ways are not my ways, nor are God's thoughts my thoughts. But where are the miracles here?

Miracles

After I recovered, I cringed every time I heard someone call my restored health a miracle. It usually came with the explanation that "God is good" and a reminder of how hard so many people had been praying for me.

What is true of any sort of medical recovery is especially true of addiction recovery. It is easy in our language to reduce recovery to simply a matter of the will. If a person believes and tries hard enough, or if those around the person pray sincerely enough, recovery will come.

Even the statement "There but for the grace of God go I," intended as an acknowledgment that you are the beneficiary of a blessing beyond your own control, can sound as if you had a special in with the person dealing the cards. I admit that I have a sore spot with that sort of language. It seems a contradiction at its core.

There are instances of recovery from addiction or disease that seem to happen instantaneously, as if by immediate and direct divine intervention. But these sorts of changes are unpredictable, have no consistent cause, and are not correlated with a specific religious doctrine or belief system.

Yet I remain drawn to the language of miracle. I am beginning to see the idea not as a contradiction but as a paradox. Miracles do not need to be mirages that dissipate as soon as the curtain is drawn back, revealing that the great and powerful Oz is neither very great nor very powerful. They do not need to be reduced to a sort of spiritual placebo effect.

I believe that there is, as Martin Buber wrote, a joining of "will and grace." Miracle is the word we give to their mysterious intersection. They are the moments of life that draw us into a relation with the world and others that could not exist otherwise.

Miracles are not the things that we don't understand and so to which we ascribe some incorporeal cause. Instead, miracles are the acknowledgment that God surrounds us and is beyond us and sometimes breaks through in ways that, at least at first, just don't make sense. What if a miracle is invoked not as the

explanation for a particular event but as a lens of hope and
grace through which we view the world?

"Thy life is a miracle. Speak yet again." These are the words
Edgar speaks to his father, the Earl of Gloucester, in Shake-
speare's *King Lear*.

Gloucester had been made blind as a consequence for his
loyalty to the king and had pushed away his faithful son Edgar.
Edgar came to his father's side in disguise. The earl asked the
disguised Edgar to lead him to the edge of the cliff so that he
might take his own life. Edgar told his father they were at
the edge, and the earl fainted as he threw himself off it.

But of course, the son had led his father not to the cliff's edge
but to the top of a small rock near the cliffs. When Gloucester
awoke, his son pretended that the earl had truly fallen from
the cliff and had survived anyway. That's when he spoke the
words: "Thy life is a miracle. Speak yet again."

It wasn't a miracle that the earl had survived. That had a
simple explanation. But Edgar was speaking a deeper truth,
one that his father needed to hear.

While we are unable to explain the tragedy that befalls us
as humans, we can still affirm life. The search for "the meaning of life"—any accounting for all the ways we have hurt or
suffered—is a fruitless quest. Victor Frankl wrote of his time
in a concentration camp, "We needed to stop asking about the
meaning of life, and instead to think of ourselves as those who
were being questioned by life—daily and hourly."[1]

The miracle of life is found in the fact that even amid great
suffering, we are able to find and create meaning. That meaning,
as Frankl noted of those who were imprisoned with him, was
often what kept prisoners alive in the worst of circumstances.

The grace to see this is not handed out stingily upon the
acceptance of a particular doctrine, religious ritual, or magical
incantation. It is an everywhere and always-present miracle
that we can choose to participate in even amid pain.

Going home

My face had changed. It was thin and drawn, and my cheekbones were sticking out. I looked in my bathroom mirror and realized I was alone. For months I had been the focus of constant care and attention, and now I was back in my own apartment. There were housemates upstairs and the nurse who would visit. But now, I was alone.

Days blurred together. I developed new ways to measure time. T. S. Elliot saw life measured out by coffee spoons; for William S. Burroughs, "life measured out in eyedroppers of morphine solution."[2] For me, time was marked by those little white pills. Some days I practiced a careful restraint by the hours and amounts dictated by the label on the bottle. Other days the pills themselves, and the relief they brought, became the markers of time. Doctors' orders faded from my field of vision.

A nurse came twice a week. She would take my vitals and then draw blood from the lines hanging out of my arm. During her second visit each week, she would repeat the process but change the dressing on my arm. Every time she would apologize, because she knew it hurt. What she didn't know was how good the hurt felt. I felt a strange kind of relief when I'd wince at the sharp pain. The knives were ghosts now—no longer real and solid, but still haunting me. Still fluttering and floating about. To feel something so new and different assured me that all things change.

I was constantly cold. The heat in the house was always running, and I had borrowed an electric heater that I would turn on high. I'd crawl underneath a goose-down comforter, in pajama pants and a sweatshirt and a bathrobe, curl up, and wait for the chill to pass.

Some days I focused on every pain and discomfort. All my energy went to wondering what new thing might be wrong with me now, which old malady still active. Every ache and soar of pain would consume my mind. I took pill after pill and lay in bed and watched show after show. These days would stretch on. I found myself with nothing to do and still taking days to do it. I experienced the world through everything I lacked, all the things that were gone from me, everything I could no longer do or enjoy. All of life denied.

There are many ways that one can give up on life. There are those who choose to end it and, like Gloucester, walk up to the edge of the cliff. But when the dark winter days stretched on, my temptation was to simply not begin again and stay in the trance the pills offered. I walked up to the edge of my own cliff. Sometimes I would just sit there and imagine the feeling of falling. I would lie in my bed and let all thought and feeling drift away, as my body and soul grew increasingly numb. My chest would rise and fall, and I would feel the tickle of the knives once again. They reminded me of the long path ahead. They taunted me with the knowledge that the path might not be long at all. Blood clots, infections, and surgeries gone wrong: any moment could be an unexpected cliff not of my own seeking. Months of struggle could still end in just a few moments.

The patches and pills were there now, fighting the knives, but they couldn't convince me that life is a miracle or even that life had meaning. The patches and pills helped stop anger, helped stop depression. They kept me from feeling much of anything at all. They protected me from the reality of what my body should be feeling and suffering.

Dry bones

I started writing.

Everything I could remember from the night I first felt pain in my stomach to the day-by-day happenings of my hospital stay. I wrote down stories I had always told other people to make them laugh, and I wrote down stories I had never told anyone. I wrote prayers that came out as angry accusations and bitter questions. I wrote renunciations and denunciations of all the praises I had ever offered and beliefs I had held. It was as if a cyst had burst and was pouring out curses and questions.

Some of the pressure was relieved, but the flow continued and left its toxic touch. On the days the flood of writing came the strongest, I could see my battle was not over. I was still fighting. Wrestling. Engaged in warfare with my own spirit. Sometimes it would come out as blasphemy. Sometimes it would come out as praise.

But in any case, as I wrote, I was remembering that I could still create. I could still build, learn, and construct ideas out of air and words. Old things were gone, but new things could come. Dust returned to dust and then out of the dust new seedlings started to grow.

In those days I wrote of my troubled visions and dreams, and I grasped for meaning that could pull me out of bed. Like the prophet Ezekiel, I sometimes felt as if I were looking out over a valley of bones. If God had asked me whether I believed those dry old bones could ever live again, I would have said I did not know.

I had become as dry bones. Everything I had been before my illness stripped away. The face in the mirror strange to me. My body, my pride, my work, my ambitions, my beliefs: they had all faded. My breath had almost stopped too. With so many things now gone, what was left became clear.

My therapist told me I sounded angry. "I know," I responded.

It's okay to be angry, he explained. At the heart of all anger is either fear or sadness. The next time you feel angry, he said, don't erase the anger. Don't just make it go away with another pill. Sit with it. Get to know the anger and where it has come from.

If, he continued, you should ever be at a place where the anger begins to recede and you find yourself with a choice between being afraid and being sad, choose sadness.

I imagined Ezekiel in that valley of dry bones.

God told Ezekiel to speak, and Ezekiel spoke. The bones rattled and came together. Bone to bone, sinew and flesh. But there was not breath in their lungs.

Speak, God commanded. Once again Ezekiel spoke. The four winds came and filled the lungs of those who had once been dead. Each life, a miracle.

I waited there at the edge of Ezekiel's valley in the unknowing, the unseeing, the unfeeling. The desert was not a punishment to be feared but a journey of transformation. The first step was not hope but sadness. Sadness acknowledged the pain and the struggle—all the ways that life was still not restored. There was a strength in that sadness that was deeper than the fear of pain and death.

The journey was slow and halting. When I found I had a choice, I chose sadness and not fear. When I found I had a voice, I spoke life and not death. It was there, in that pregnant pause, that holy winter, that divine dark, that my skin began to grow. Scales on my eyes softened.

Prophecies will cease, tongues will be stilled, and knowledge will fade away. At best I will only ever see as through a glass darkly, and yet some things remain. Faith, I could still trust it. Hope, I could still choose it. Love, I could still feel it.

My life, a miracle.

24

Resurrection

On the day before Easter, my mother and I took my first extended walk outside. I had regained enough strength to fly from my home in Washington, D.C., to spend a few weeks recovering with my parents at their farm in New Hampshire.

My mom and I climbed Jim's Ridge, a steep field where you can look west and see my parents' house on the next hill. There were still patches of snow in the woods, but the sun was out and thawing the ground. The smell of last year's wet leaves beginning their journey back to the earth mingled with the fresh green growth pushing up from the ground. Even though I moved slowly, the exertion of my body and the light from above warmed me.

We talked about me being sick. She thanked God for the support she had received and that I was still alive.

I had not yet thanked God. If God was the one who healed me, then God was also the one who had allowed me to get sick in the first place. The two remained in holy opposition.

"I sure hope the sermon is good on Easter," I said to her as we stopped partway up the hill. We turned around as I caught my breath and looked at the Uncanoonuc Mountains, two peaks on the south end of town.

"Why?" my mom asked.

"I feel like it would be a good way to wrap this all up," I said, some resentment likely edging my voice. "Some divine revelation and deep spiritual lesson that puts everything in context and makes everything make sense again."

"Don't you think that is a lot of pressure to put on Pastor Joel?"

"But wouldn't that be a great end to it all?" I insisted. "Sick all winter and then everything makes sense when spring starts and we celebrate Easter."

My mom was uncertain, predicting my inevitable disappointment, but she kept her own counsel.

On Easter morning I took a seat in the church of my youth. On my way in, I had greeted old Sunday school teachers and family friends, all of whom had been praying for me, with a gratitude thinly hiding my exhaustion. My gaunt frame felt out of place and uncomfortable in the wooden pew.

I waited there with a sullen kind of anticipation. I wondered whether I should finally let go of my childish hope that the world might be better than I expected.

Stronger where we are broken

Grace points to the possibility of a redemption that is not just recovery but the opportunity to grow deeper and become stronger than we were before. The limp might be a reminder of the wrestling match. But it is never stronger than the blessing that comes as we hold on.

Kintsugi is a form of Japanese pottery repair. A broken clay bowl is not disposed of but instead is re-created using precious metals, often gold. The result is a vessel with beautiful scars and a strength greater than before.

This image of a repaired bowl is not just a metaphor. As discussed earlier, over time, severe addiction reduces the amount of gray matter in the part of our brain most responsible for higher-level reasoning and self-control. A 2013 study of the brains of those struggling with cocaine addiction suggests something interesting. Within a few months of sobriety, that gray matter began to return. Within six to twelve months, the gray matter had returned to baseline levels and was about the same as those who had never been addicted. But soon after that is when the most amazing thing happened: those areas began to form an even greater level of density than for those who had never used cocaine.[1]

"Frequently, an addiction or an attachment—once we recognize it—catapults us on a path to healing, which we would not otherwise have pursued," write Frances Kelly Nemeck and Marie Theresa Coombs. "It is as if the fixation is a symptom of an inner woundedness crying out for redemption. The fixation of our will is like a warning signal amplified to peak intensity, demanding that we deal with the inner hurt or deprivation."[2]

I do not mean to glamorize the addictive experience. The hurt and destruction it can cause is great. Not all harm can be repaired with gold seams, nor all relationships be strengthened at the points at which they were fractured by addiction.

We are born into a world filled with both grace and tragedy. We are thrown into a life we did not choose. We carry early wounds from those who were themselves wounded before us. Those wounds can be hardened into weapons that we use to defend ourselves and, in the process, wound others. Or we can turn those wounds into seams of grace.

Grace is found in the reality that our pain is not the entire story. The patterns of being hurt and hurting others can be interrupted. We do not need to live in a downward cascade of violence; we can interrupt it. As Richard Rohr says, "If we do not transform our pain, we will most assuredly transmit it."[3]

The wealth in much of the world today can make it easy to forget our constant need. The things we consume are enough to provide an illusion that we are self-sufficient and can supply all the things we need. Addiction is the force that reveals how wrong we are.

It would be a mistake to conclude that grace is present only in a complete sobriety. Our lives will always have relapses, setbacks, and new mistakes. We will always maintain some vestige of the old even as we step into the new. Grace resides not only in the moment that someone finally overcomes an addiction. Grace is present in every small step, in any positive change, and, miraculously, even in the wrong choices.

Julian of Norwich wrote, "First the fall and then the recovery from the fall, and both are the mercy of God."[4] Grace is on display in every step toward healing—and grace is still present in the choices that bend toward addiction.

What we think about addiction says a lot about what we think of those who are addicted. And when each of us is addicted in our own way, we learn a lot about how we think of and experience ourselves. The exploration of addiction in a nation and culture is not just an external searching but a path of internal discovery.

We have been in the desert of this overdose crisis for forty years, even if we didn't always know it. Silence and shame, scapegoating and blame have all hidden the true nature of the epidemic from ourselves and allowed it to grow. Are we ready to break from our collective denial that addiction is not just an individual challenge but a social, political, economic, and spiritual one?

Not the end

A few minutes into the Easter service, a woman got up and read the Easter Scripture. She read the story I'd heard countless times before: about the women rising early on that Sabbath morning, going to Jesus' tomb, and finding it empty.

Partway through the story, I suddenly realized the personalized message I had been seeking wasn't coming. I took a sharp breath: it takes a special kind of egocentricity to believe that my situation was so unique that God needed to say new words to me. To believe that I had suffered in such a way that a new story needed to be told. That I would find a resolution others hadn't. What would make me so privileged that, in the middle of my life, pain and miracles and illness and grace and addiction and freedom would suddenly make sense? Why should I receive special dispensation, such that all inconsistencies of existence would be resolved, all theological confusion cleared up, all human pain understood?

As I sat on that hard pew, I realized the most important message that I will ever hear I had already heard. I realized, too, that I was only one of several billion people in the world who would hear it. This message is what Job understood as his life, family, and fortune were devastated and then restored. This word was in Jacob's wrestling, and in Mary Magdalene's tears at an empty grave. It was in Wilberforce's work for freedom amid his own bondage and all the mothers who have turned the pain of their loss into a campaign for healing. It is a significant message precisely because it is *not* new. This story is relatable because it is messy, confusing, and sometimes even incomplete. It is so powerful because it is a story not just for me but for everyone and anyone.

The message is this: death is not the final resolution. When pain racks our bodies, this is not the end. When we feel beaten, ready to give up the fight, and gasp in thirst, this is not the end. When the cry leaves our lips, "Why have you forsaken me?" this is not the end. When our hearts stop beating and lungs fail, this is not the end. When the spear pierces our side and the blood and water flow separately, this is not the end. When the earth quakes, the curtain tears, and the walls begin to crumble, this is not the end. When days go by and we feel foolish for having waited, this is not the end. When we go to the tomb, unsure of what we'll find, this is not the end.

The end is an empty grave.

When we know the end of the story—that death loses and resurrection wins—then we can trust that while forces beyond our control bend and sway our lives, they do not need to break them. We can decide what kind of habits and practices we want to define both our individual lives and our lives together. When we know the end is an empty grave, we can receive the goodness of the world while pursuing the vision of a better world that together we can imagine. When we are transformed by the grace of the resurrection, we can walk through the desert and know that it is not wasted time but the ground of new life.

Christ's resurrection story has been read countless times and has provided comfort, inspiration, and strength to a great cloud of witnesses. It is an invitation to a different foundation than we're used to. It is not just a new program for happiness but an entirely different kind of operating system. The resurrection calls us to put on "the mind of Christ," and to see that it is in the middle of being empty that we can be filled. It is in being brought low that we can rise, and it is in losing our life that we can find new life.

Listening to the Easter story that morning in the church of my childhood, I realized that it was not just a story of something that happened long ago and far away—although it is also that. The fundamental shape of the reality is the cross and resurrection. Resurrection, as Wendell Berry put it, is something we practice.

The resurrection of Christ reveals something about the very nature of all existence. It is a story that declares that the fundamental structure of the universe is deeper than cause and effect. That we are more than our biology. That meaning lies deeper than what can be measured, counted, or reported. That truth can be true even when it is mysterious.

The overdose crisis is not the end if we can see what it reveals about us, if we commit to right the wrongs of our past and present and work to make things whole. Addiction, both personal and communal, can be transformed into a learning that makes us stronger than before.

That even when we feel as if we are falling apart, and sometimes because we are, new life is possible for us and our world.

Acknowledgments

I'd like to thank my wife, Hannah. You've been an amazing thought partner and editor throughout this entire process. I wouldn't have even finished the first article let alone this book without you.

My love and gratitude to my mom, dad, and the rest of the family for keeping me alive. And to my older sister, Bethany, my first debating partner, for improving my thinking and for all your feedback on early drafts and research.

To Jim Wallis, Joan Bisset, Heather Wilson, and the entire Sojourners family for all the support and care during my hospital stay and recovery. For my unnamed doctor and that critical moment of empathy and compassion.

Many thanks to Bill Miller for the time and insight into my own addiction story and the process of recovery.

For my friends and early readers: Stephen Smith, Rayshauna Gray, and Drew Cleveland.

For the votes of early confidence in this project from Richard Rohr, Scot McKnight, and Timothy Johnson.

Thanks to my agent, Angela Scheff, and The Christopher Ferebee Agency for helping make this book a reality. And to Valerie Weaver-Zercher and the whole team at Herald Press who saw that my story could become a book before I did and then edited this thing into existence.

Notes

Chapter 1

1. Keegan Hamilton, "America's New Deadliest Drug Is Fentanyl," Vice News, last modified August 30, 2016, https://news.vice.com/en_us/ article/ev998e/americas-new-deadliest-drug-fentanyl.

2. Cameron Knight, "Ohio Officer Needed 4 Doses of Naloxone after Being Exposed to Fentanyl," *Cincinnati Enquirer*, last modified March 12, 2018, https://www.cincinnati.com/story/news/crime/crime-and-courts/2018/03/12/ohio-officer-needed-4-doses-naloxone-after-being-exposed-fentanyl/418395002/.

3. Sarah Jorgensen, "Fentanyl Seizure Had Enough Doses to Poison All of NYC and New Jersey," Cable News Network, last modified January 29, 2018, https://www.cnn.com/2018/01/29/health/nj-largest-fentanyl-seizure-trnd/index.html.

4. Artemis Moshtaghian, "Police Officer Overdoses after Brushing Fentanyl Powder Off His Uniform," Cable News Network, last modified May 16, 2017, https://www.cnn.com/2017/05/16/health/police-fentanyl-overdose-trnd/index.html.

5. Susan Green, "Hotspot Study Shines New Light on the Granite State's Opioid Crisis," Dartmouth Geisel School of Medicine News, last modified August 23, 2017, https://geiselmed.dartmouth.edu/news/ 2017/hotspot-study-shines-new-light-on-the-granite-states-opioid-crisis/.

6. National Center on Health Statistics, "National Overdose Deaths from Select Prescription and Illicit Drugs," CDC Wonder (provisional 2017 data), accessed March 3, 2019, https://www.drugabuse.gov/ sites/default/files/overdose-data.xls.

7. Holly Hedegaard, Margaret Warner, and Arialdi M. Miniño, "Drug
    Overdose Deaths in the United States, 1999–2016," NCHS Data Brief
    294, December 2017, https://www.cdc.gov/nchs/products/databriefs/
    db294.htm.
8. Jimmy Carter, "Crisis of Confidence" (speech), July 15, 1979,
    Miller Center of Public Affairs, University of Virginia, transcript
    and MP4 video, 33:05, https://millercenter.org/the-presidency/
    presidential-speeches/july-15-1979-crisis-confidence-speech.
9. Hawre Jalal et al., "Changing Dynamics of the Drug Overdose
    Epidemic in the United States from 1979 through 2016," *Science*,
    September 21, 2018, https://doi.org/10.1126/science.aau1184.
10. National Center on Health Statistics, "National Overdose Deaths."
11. Gerald May, *Addiction and Grace* (San Francisco: HarperSanFran-
    cisco, 1991), 11.

Chapter 2

1. Francis Seeburger, *Addiction and Responsibility: An Inquiry into
    the Addictive Mind* (CreateSpace Independent Publishing Platform,
    2013), ch. 1, loc. 207–12, Kindle.
2. Gerald May, *Addiction and Grace* (San Francisco: HarperSanFran-
    cisco, 1991), 3.
3. Peg O'Connor, *Life on the Rocks: Finding Meaning in Addiction and
    Recovery* (Las Vegas: Central Recovery Press, 2016), 8.
4. Frank Schalow, *Toward a Phenomenology of Addiction: Embodi-
    ment, Technology, Transcendence*, Contributions to Phenomenology
    93 (Geneva: Springer International, 2017), 4.

Chapter 3

1. "Definition of Addiction," American Society of Addiction Medicine,
    April 12, 2011, https://www.asam.org/resources/definition-of-
    addiction.
2. Caroline Jean Acker, "The Junkie as Psychopath," chap. 7 in *Creat-
    ing the American Junkie: Addiction Research in the Classic Era of
    Narcotic Control* (Baltimore: Johns Hopkins University Press, 2002).
3. "ASAM Releases New Definition of Addiction," American Society of
    Addiction Medicine, August 15, 2011, https://www.asam.org/docs/
    pressreleases/asam-definition-of-addiction-2011-08-15.pdf.
4. Ibid.

5. W. R. Miller et al., "What Predicts Relapse? Prospective Testing of Antecedent Models," supplement, *Addiction* 91 (December 1996): S155–72.

6. Quoted in "William Wilberforce," *Christianity Today*, accessed September 9, 2018, https://www.christianitytoday.com/history/people/activists/william-wilberforce.html.

7. Ibid.

8. *Online Etymology Dictionary*, s.v. "addiction," accessed March 3, 2019, https://www.etymonline.com/word/addict.

Chapter 4

1. Sam Quinones, *Dreamland: The True Tale of America's Opiate Epidemic* (New York: Bloomsbury, 2016), 286.

2. Beth Macy, *Dopesick: Dealers, Doctors, and the Drug Company That Addicted America* (New York: Little, Brown and Company, 2018), 8.

3. Ibid., 141.

4. Ibid., 241.

5. Audre Lorde, *Sister Outsider* (New York: Random House, 2012), 41.

Chapter 5

1. Hannah Pickard, "Responsibility without Blame," chap. 66 in *Oxford Handbook of Philosophy and Psychiatry*, ed. K. W. M. Fulford et al. (Oxford: Oxford University Press, 2013).

2. Hafiz, "The Sad Game," in *The Gift: Poems by Hafiz the Great Sufi Master*, trans. Daniel Ladinsky (New York: Penguin Group, 1999), 117.

3. James Cone, *The Cross and the Lynching Tree* (Maryknoll, NY: Orbis Books, 2012), xv.

Chapter 6

1. Martin Booth, *Opium: A History* (New York: St. Martin's Press, 1999), 85.

2. David T. Courtwright, *Dark Paradise: A History of Opiate Addiction* (Cambridge, MA: Harvard University Press, 2001), introduction, loc. 105, Kindle.

3. Maia Szalavitz, "What the Media Gets Wrong about Opioids," *Columbia Journalism Review*, last modified August 15, 2018, https://

www.cjr.org/covering_the_health_care_fight/what-the-media-gets-wrong-about-opioids.php.

4. Craig Reinarman and Harry G. Levine, ed., *Crack in America: Demon Drugs and Social Justice* (Berkeley: University of California Press, 1997), 1.

5. Ibid., 3.

6. Ibid., 27. Emphasis in the original.

7. Ibid., 2.

8. Michelle Alexander, *The New Jim Crow: Mass Incarceration in the Age of Colorblindness* (New York: The New Press, 2010), 51.

9. Ibid.

10. Ibid., 56.

11. Ed Stetzer, "'Lock Them Up': My Double Standard in Responding to the Crack Crisis vs. the Opioid Epidemic," *Washington Post*, October 26, 2017, https://www.washingtonpost.com/news/acts-of-faith/wp/2017/10/26/lock-them-up-my-double-standard-in-responding-to-the-crack-crisis-vs-the-opioid-epidemic/?noredirect=on&utm_term=.7482f25bc633.

12. Ibid.

13. Brian Broome, "Amid the Opioid Epidemic, White Means Victim, Black Means Addict," *The Guardian*, April 28, 2018, https://www.theguardian.com/us-news/2018/apr/28/opioid-epidemic-selects-white-victim-black-addict.

14. Julie Netherland and Helena Hansen, "The War on Drugs That Wasn't: Wasted Whiteness, 'Dirty Doctors,' and Race in Media Coverage of Prescription Opioid Misuse," *Culture, Medicine, and Psychiatry* 40, no. 4 (2016): 664–86.

15. Helena Hansen and Julie Netherland, "Is the Prescription Opioid Epidemic a White Problem?, *American Journal of Public Health* 106, no. 12 (2016): 2127–29.

16. National Center on Health Statistics, "National Overdose Deaths from Select Prescription and Illicit Drugs," CDC Wonder (provisional 2017 data), accessed March 3, 2019, https://www.drugabuse.gov/sites/default/files/overdose-data.xls.

17. Bruce Wilshire, *Wild Hunger: The Primal Roots of Modern Addiction* (Lanham, MD: Rowman and Littlefield, 1999), 195.

18. Courtwright, *Dark Paradise*, chap. 2, loc. 775–76.

19. Ibid., chap. 2, loc. 776–77.

Chapter 7

1. Anne Case and Angus Deaton, "Rising Midlife Morbidity and Mortality, US Whites," *Proceedings of the National Academy of Sciences* 112, no. 49 (December 2015): 15078–83, https://doi.org/10.1073/pnas.1518393112.

2. Karl Clifton-Soderstrom, *The Cardinal and the Deadly* (Eugene, OR: Cascade Books, 2105), 32.

3. Anne Case and Angus Deaton, "Mortality and Morbidity in the 21st Century," *Brookings Papers on Economic Activity*, Spring 2017, 397, https://www.brookings.edu/wp-content/uploads/2017/08/casetextsp17bpea.pdf.

4. Ibid., 423.

5. Susan Glasser and Glenn Thrush, "What's Going on with America's White People?," *Politico*, September-October 2016, https://www.politico.com/magazine/story/2016/09/problems-white-people-america-society-class-race-214227, quoted in Case and Deaton, "Mortality and Morbidity," 429.

6. Quoted in Clifton-Soderstrom, *The Cardinal and the Deadly*, 32.

7. Albert Camus, *The Myth of Sisyphus: And Other Essays*, trans. Justin O'Brien (New York: Vintage International, 2012), 121. First published 1955.

8. Kent Dunnington, *Addiction and Virtue: Beyond the Models of Disease and Choice*, Strategic Initiatives in Evangelical Theology (Downers Grove, IL: IVP Academic, 2012), chap. 5, loc. 1181–82, Kindle.

9. Camus, *The Myth of Sisyphus*, 123.

10. Jimmy Carter, "Crisis of Confidence" (speech), July 15, 1979, Miller Center of Public Affairs, University of Virginia, transcript and MP4 video, 33:05, https://millercenter.org/the-presidency/presidential-speeches/july-15-1979-crisis-confidence-speech.

Chapter 8

1. Gabor Maté, *In the Realm of Hungry Ghosts: Close Encounters with Addiction* (Berkeley, CA: North Atlantic Books, 2009), 35.

2. Elaine Scarry, *The Body in Pain: The Making and Unmaking of the World* (New York: Oxford University Press, 1985), 7.

Chapter 9

1. Walter Wink, *The Powers That Be* (New York: Harmony, 2010), 31.

2. Sam Quinones, *Dreamland: The True Tale of America's Opiate Epidemic* (New York: Bloomsbury Publishing, 2016), 82.

3. Eric Eyre, "Drug Firms Shipped 20.8M Pain Pills to WV Town with 2,900 People," *Charleston Gazette-Mail*, January 29, 2018, https://www.wvgazettemail.com/news/health/drug-firms-shipped-m-pain-pills-to-wv-town-with/article_ef04190c-1763-5a0c-a77a-7da0ff06455b.html.

4. Quinones, *Dreamland*, 134.

5. On number who experience chronic pain and the estimated costs: IOM (Institute of Medicine), *Relieving Pain in America: A Blueprint for Transforming Prevention, Care, Education, and Research* (Washington, DC: National Academics Press, 2011), 2, http://www.nationalacademies.org/hmd/Reports/2011/Relieving-Pain-in-America-A-Blueprint-for-Transforming-Prevention-Care-Education-Research.aspx; on those experiencing daily chronic pain: Richard L. Nahin, "Estimates of Pain Prevalence and Severity in Adults: United States," *Journal of Pain* 16, no. 8 (August 2015): 769, https://doi.org/10.1016/j.jpain.2015.05.002.

6. IOM, *Relieving Pain*, 194, 198.

7. Wink, *The Powers That Be*, 2.

8. Thomas Merton, *New Seeds of Contemplation* (Halifax, NS: Shambhala, 2003), 33–34.

9. James Finley, *Merton's Palace of Nowhere* (Notre Dame, IN: Ave Maria Press, 2017), 5. First published 1978.

Chapter 10

1. Ronald Siegel, *Intoxication: The Universal Drive for Mind-Altering Substances* (Rochester, VT: Park Street Press, 2005), 126.

2. Martin Booth, *Opium: A History* (New York: St. Martin's Press, 1999), 15.

3. Ibid., 17.

4. Ibid., 19.

5. Ibid., 20.

6. Sam Quinones, *Dreamland: The True Tale of America's Opiate Epidemic* (New York: Bloomsbury Publishing, 2016), 52.

7. Anil Aggrawal, "The Story of Opium," chap. 2 in *Narcotic Drugs* (New Deli: National Book Trust, 1995), https://www.opioids.com/narcotic-drugs/chapter-2.html.

8. Quoted in David T. Courtwright, *Dark Paradise: A History of Opiate Addiction* (Cambridge, MA: Harvard University Press, 2001), chap. 2, loc. 548–50, Kindle.

9. Booth, *Opium: A History*, 65.

10. Courtwright, *Dark Paradise*, chap. 2, loc. 619–20.

11. Craig Reinarman and Harry G. Levine, eds., *Crack in America: Demon Drugs and Social Justice* (Berkeley: University of California Press, 1997), 8–9.

12. Dr. Nora Volkow, director of the National Institute on Drug Abuse, published a review in the *New England Journal of Medicine* arguing that in studies where addiction is carefully defined, addiction rates for prescribed opioids average less than 8 percent, and a broader definition of misuse and broader "addiction-related" behaviors brings the average to somewhere between 15 and 26 percent. See Nora D. Volkow and A. Thomas McLellan, "Opioid Abuse and Chronic Pain—Misconceptions and Mitigation Strategies," *New England Journal of Medicine*, March 31, 2016, https://www.nejm .org/doi/ full/10.1056/nejmra1507771.

13. Christopher C. H. Cook, *Alcohol, Addiction and Christian Ethics* (Cambridge, UK: University of Cambridge Press, 2005), 119.

14. Quoted in Reinarman and Levine, *Crack in America*, 6.

15. "Alcohol and Public Health: Fact Sheets: Alcohol Use and Your Health," Centers for Disease Control and Prevention, last modified January 3, 2018, https://www.cdc.gov/alcohol/fact-sheets/alcohol-use .htm.

16. Gabor Maté, *In the Realm of Hungry Ghosts: Close Encounters with Addiction* (Berkeley, CA: North Atlantic Books, 2009), 158–60.

17. Ibid., 162.

Chapter 11

1. Gabor Maté, *In the Realm of Hungry Ghosts: Close Encounters with Addiction* (Berkeley, CA: North Atlantic Books, 2009), 137.

2. Ibid., 150.

3. *Essays of Montaigne*, trans. Charles Cotton, ed. William Carew Hazlitt (London: Reeves and Turner, 1877), 2:392.

4. William Irvine, *On Desire: Why We Want What We Want* (Oxford: Oxford University Press, 2006), 95.

5. Richard O'Connor, *Rewire: Change Your Brain to Break Bad Habits, Overcome Addictions, Conquer Self-Destructing Behavior* (New York: Penguin Random House, 2014), 1.

6. Neil Levy, "Addiction and Self-Control: Perspectives from Philosophy, Psychology, and Neuroscience," in *Addiction and Self-Control: Perspectives from Philosophy, Psychology, and Neuroscience*, ed. Neil Levy (Oxford: Oxford University Press, 2013), 11.

7. Ibid.

8. M. Price, "Genes Matter in Addiction," *Monitor on Psychology* 39, no. 6 (June 2008): 14, https://www.apa.org/monitor/2008/06/genes-addict.aspx.

Chapter 12

1. Alvin M. Shuster, "G.I. Heroin Addiction Epidemic in Vietnam," *New York Times*, May 16, 1971, available at https://www.nytimes.com/1971/05/16/archives/gi-heroin-addiction-epidemic-in-vietnam-gi-heroin-addiction-is.html.

2. Lee N. Robins, Darlene H. Davis, and David N. Nurco, "How Permanent Was Vietnam Drug Addiction?" *AJPH Supplement* 64 (December 1974): 38–43, https://ajph.aphapublications.org/doi/pdf/10.2105/AJPH.64.12_Suppl.38.

3. Neil Levy, "Addiction Is Not a Brain Disease (and It Matters)," *Frontiers in Psychiatry* 4, no. 24. (2013), https://doi.org/10.3389/fpsyt.2013.00024.

4. Bruce K. Alexander, *The Globalization of Addiction: A Study in Poverty of the Spirit* (Oxford: Oxford University Press, 2008), introduction, loc. 135–36, Kindle.

5. Ibid., chap. 8, loc. 3988–93.

6. Andre B. Rosay, "Violence against American Indian and Alaska Native Men and Women," *National Institute of Justice Research Report May 2016* (Washington, DC: U.S. Department of Justice, 2016), 11, https://www.ncjrs.gov/pdffiles1/nij/249736.pdf.

7. Alexander, *The Globalization of Addiction*, loc. 2640–42.

8. Ibid., chap. 6, loc. 2681–726.

9. Mikyta Daugherty et al., "Substance Abuse among Displaced and Indigenous Peoples," in *Changing Substance Abuse through Health and Social Systems*, ed. William R. Miller and Constance M. Weisner (New York: Kluwer Academic, 2002), 233.

10. Alexander, *The Globalization of Addiction*, chap. 6, loc. 2667–74.

Chapter 13

1. Sam Quinones, *Dreamland: The True Tale of America's Opiate Epidemic* (New York: Bloomsbury Publishing, 2016), 52.

2. Quoted in Martin Booth, *Opium: A History* (New York: St. Martin's Press), 69.

3. Martin Heidegger, *The Question concerning Technology and Other Essays*, trans. William Lovitt (New York: Harper, 1977), 4.

4. Steve Sussman, Nadra Lisha, and Mark D. Griffiths, "Prevalence of the Addictions: A Problem of the Majority or the Minority?," *Evaluation and the Health Professions* 34 (2011): 3–56.

5. Adam Alter, *Irresistible: The Rise of Addictive Technology and the Business of Keeping Us Hooked* (New York: Penguin, 2017), 9.

6. Renée Descartes, *Discourse on the Method of Rightly Conducting One's Reason and Seeking Truth in the Sciences*, in the version by Jonathan Bennett presented at EarlyModernTexts.com, 12, https://www.earlymoderntexts.com/assets/pdfs/descartes1637.pdf.

Chapter 14

1. Francis Seeburger, *Addiction and Responsibility: An Inquiry into the Addictive Mind* (CreateSpace Independent Publishing Platform, 2013), ch 1, loc. 374–76, Kindle.

2. Marc Lewis, *The Biology of Desire: Why Addiction Is Not a Disease* (New York: PublicAffairs), 73.

3. Ibid., 142.

4. Timothy Brewerton and Amy Dennis, eds., *Eating Disorders, Addictions and Substance Use Disorders* (Berlin: Springer-Verlag, 2014); Nora Volkow et al., "The Addictive Dimensionality of Obesity," *Biological Psychiatry* 73, no. 9 (2013): 811–18, https://doi.org/10.1016/j.biopsych.2012.12.020.

5. Saki Knafo, "Change of Habit: How Seattle Cops Fought an Addiction to Locking Up Drug Users," *Huffington Post*, last modified December 6, 2017, https://www.huffingtonpost.com/2014/08/28/seattle-lead-program_n_5697660.html.

6. Thomas Merton, *Conjectures of a Guilty Bystander* (New York: Image Books, 2009), 153–55. First published 1965.

7. Ralph Waldo Emerson, *Emerson: The Ultimate Collection* (Titan Read, 2015), ch. 10, loc. 3143, Kindle.

Chapter 15

1. Kent Dunnington, *Addiction and Virtue: Beyond the Models of Disease and Choice Strategic Initiatives in Evangelical Theology* (Downers Grove, IL: IVP Academic, 2012), ch. 2, loc. 272–73, Kindle.
2. Ibid., ch. 3, loc. 608–9.
3. Quoted in ibid., ch. 3, loc. 698–702.
4. Ibid.
5. Quoted in Bruce Wilshire, *Wild Hunger: The Primal Roots of Modern Addiction* (Lanham, MD: Rowman and Littlefield, 1999), 74–75. Emphasis in the original.
6. Candace B. Pert, *Molecules of Emotion: The Science behind Mind-Body Medicine* (New York: Touchstone, 1999), 187. First published 1997.
7. Matthias Pierce et al., "Impact of Treatment for Opioid Dependence on Fatal Drug-Related Poisoning: A National Cohort Study in England," *Addiction* 111, no. 2 (February 2016): 298, https://doi.org/10.1111/add.13193.

Chapter 16

1. Jean-Paul Sartre, *Being and Nothingness*, trans. H. Barnes (New York: Washington Square Press, 1956), 58.

Chapter 17

1. Samuel Taylor Coleridge, *Christabel; Kubla Khan: a Vision; The Pains of Sleep* (London: 1816).
2. Johann Hari, *Chasing the Scream: The First and Last Days of the War on Drugs* (New York: Bloomsbury Publishing, 2015), ch. 13, loc. 3301–4, Kindle.
3. J. K. Zubieta et al., "Placebo Effects Mediated by Endogenous Opioid Activity on Mu-opioid Receptors," *Journal of Neuroscience* 25, no. 34 (August 24, 2005): 7754–62, cited in Gabor Maté, *In the Realm of Hungry Ghosts: Close Encounters with Addiction* (Berkeley, CA: North Atlantic Books, 2009), 160.
4. Francis Seeburger, *Addiction and Responsibility: An Inquiry into the Addictive Mind* (CreateSpace Independent Publishing Platform, 2013), ch.1, loc. 302–4, Kindle.
5. Ibid., ch. 1, loc. 304–7.

6. Carl Jung to William G.W.–, January 30th, 1961, quoted in David E. Schoen, *The War of the Gods in Addiction* (New Orleans: Spring Journal Books, 2012), ch. 1, loc. 369–87.
7. Martin Booth, *Opium: A History* (New York: St. Martin's Press, 1999), 26.

Chapter 18

1. Scot McKnight, *Sermon on the Mount*, The Story of God Bible Commentary (Grand Rapids, MI: Zondervan, 2013), ch. 10, loc. 3469–70, Kindle.
2. Ibid., ch. 10, loc 3623.
3. Jean-Luc Marion, "The Idol and the Icon," chap. 1 in *God without Being* (Chicago: University of Chicago Press, 1991).
4. Paraphrased from Nikos Kazantzakis, *Zorba the Greek*, trans. Carl Widman (London: Faber and Faber, 1959).
5. Rainer Maria Rilke, *Rilke's Book of Hours: Love Poems to God*, trans. Anita Barrows and Joanna Macy (New York: Riverhead, 1996), 48.

Chapter 19

1. William R. Miller and Stephen Rollnick, *Motivational Interviewing: Helping People Change*, 3rd ed. (New York: Guilford Press, 2013), 4.
2. Maia Szalavitz documents some of the worst abuses aimed at young people in her book *Help at Any Cost: How the Troubled-Teen Industry Cons Parents and Hurts Kids* (New York: Riverhead Books, 2006).
3. William L. White and William R. Miller, "The Use of Confrontation in Addiction Treatment: History, Science, and Time for Change," *Counselor* 8, no. 4 (August 2007): 24–25.
4. William R. Miller and Theresa B. Moyers, "The Forest and the Trees: Relational and Specific Factors in Addiction Treatment," *Addiction* 110, no. 3 (2014): 401–13, https://doi.org/10.1111/add.12693.
5. Pierre Teilhard de Chardin, "Patient Trust," in *Hearts on Fire: Praying with Jesuits*, ed. Michael Hater (Chicago: Loyola, 1993), 102.
6. Ibid.

Chapter 20

1. Francis Seeburger, *Addiction and Responsibility: An Inquiry into the Addictive Mind* (CreateSpace Independent Publishing Platform, 2013), ch. 7, loc. 1971–73, Kindle.
2. Karl Clifton-Soderstrom, *The Cardinal and the Deadly: Reimagining the Seven Virtues and Seven Vices* (New York: Cascade Books), 42.
3. George Ainslie, "Money as MacGuffin: A Factor in Gambling and Other Process Addictions," in *Addiction and Self-Control: Perspectives from Philosophy, Psychology, and Neuroscience*, ed. Neil Levy (Oxford: Oxford University Press, 2013), 22.
4. Bruce Wilshire, *Wild Hunger: The Primal Roots of Modern Addiction* (Lanham, MD: Rowman and Littlefield, 1999), 10.
5. Ibid., 257.
6. Ibid., 258.

Chapter 21

1. George J. Leake and Albert S. King, "Effect of Counselor Expectations on Alcoholic Recovery," *Alcohol Health and Research World* 1 (1977): 16–22.
2. William R. Miller, *Lovingkindness: Realizing and Practicing Your True Self* (New York: Cascade Books, 2017), 44.
3. William R. Miller, "Rediscovering Fire: Small Interventions, Large Effects," *Psychology of Addictive Behaviors* 14, no. 1 (2000): 6–18, https://doi.org/10.1037//0893-164X.14.1.6.
4. Susan Milmoe et al., "The Doctor's Voice: Postdictor of Successful Referral of Alchoholic Patients," *Journal of Abnormal Psychology*, 72, no. 1: 78–84, http://dx.doi.org/10.1037/h0024219.
5. Walter Brueggemann, *The Prophetic Imagination* (Minneapolis: Fortress Press, 1978), 40.
6. Ibid.
7. Howard Thurman, *Meditations of the Heart* (Boston: Beacon Press, 2014), 37.
8. Noya Galai et al., "Longitudinal Patterns of Drug Injection Behavior in the ALIVE Study Cohort, 1988–2000: Description and Determinants," *American Journal of Epidemiology* 158, no. 7 (2003): 695–704, https://doi.org/10.1093/aje/kwg209.
9. A. Aizer and J. J. Doyle, "Juvenile Incarceration and Adult Outcomes: Evidence from Randomly-Assigned Judges," National Bureau of Economic Research, February 2011, https://www.law.yale.edu/system/

files/area/workshop/leo/document/J.Doyle.swingjudges_03032011
.pdf.

10. UK Home Office, "Drugs: International Comparators," October
     2014, accessed March 3, 2019, https://www.gov.uk/government/
     uploads/system/uploads/attachment_data/file/368489/Drugs
     InternationalComparators.pdf.

11. European Monitoring Centre for Drugs and Drug Addiction (2017),
     Portugal, Country Drug Report 2017, Publications Office of the
     European Union, Luxembourg, http://www.emcdda.europa.eu/system/
     files/publications/4508/TD0116918ENN.pdf.

12. European Monitoring Centre for Drugs and Drug Addiction (2017),
     European Drug Report 2017: Trends and Developments, Publications
     Office of the European Union, Luxembourg; Holly Hedegaard,
     Arialdi M. Miniño, and Margaret Warner, "Drug Overdose Deaths
     in the United States, 1999–2017," NCHS Data Brief 329, November
     2018, https://www.cdc.gov/nchs/data/databriefs/db329-h.pdf.

13. Quoted in Nigel Hawkes, "Highs and Lows of Drug Decriminal-
     ization," *The BMJ* 343, no. 7829 (2011): d6881, https://doi.org/10
     .1136.bmj.d6881.

14. Richard Rohr, *Breathing Under Water: Spirituality and the Twelve
     Steps* (Cincinnati: St. Anthony Messenger Press, 2011), introduction,
     loc. 230, Kindle.

Chapter 22

1. Gerald May, *Addiction and Grace* (San Francisco: HarperSanFran-
    cisco, 1991), 4.

2. Ibid., 52.

3. William R. Miller, "Rediscovering Fire: Small Interventions, Large
    Effects," *Psychology of Addictive Behaviors* 14, no. 1 (2000): 11,
    https://doi.org/10.1037//0893-164X.14.1.6.

4. William R. Miller and Stephen Rollnick, preface to *Motivational
    Interviewing: Helping People Change*, 3rd ed. (New York: Guilford
    Press, 2013), viii.

5. Pierre Teilhard de Chardin, *Toward the Future* (New York: Harcourt
    Brace Jovanovich, 1975), 87, cited in Miller, "Rediscovering Fire," 16.

6. Owen Flanagan, "The Epistemic Authority of Alcoholics Anony-
    mous," in *Addiction and Self-Control: Perspectives from Philosophy,
    Psychology, and Neuroscience*, ed. Neil Levy (Oxford: Oxford
    University Press, 2013), ch 5.

7. Zhiling Zou et al., "Romantic Love vs. Drug Addiction May Inspire a New Treatment for Addiction," *Frontiers in Psychology* 7 (September 2016): 1436, https://doi.org/10.3389/fpsyg.2016.01436.

Chapter 23

1. Victor Frankl, *Man's Search For Meaning* (New York: Pocket Books, 1985), 98.
2. William S. Burroughs, *Junky: The Definitive Text of "Junk"* (New York: Grove Atlantic, 2003), 5–6. First published 1953.

Chapter 24

1. Colm G. Connolly et al., "Dissociated Grey Matter Changes with Prolonged Addiction and Extended Abstinence in Cocaine Users," *PLoS ONE* 8, no. 3 (March 2013): e59645, https://doi.org/10.1371/journal.pone.0059645.
2. Francis Kelly Nemeck and Marie Theresa Coombs, *O Blessed Night: Recovering from Addiction, Codependency and Attachment Based on the Insights of St. John of the Cross and Pierre Teilhard de Chardin* (Staten Island, NY: Alba House, 1991), 53.
3. Richard Rohr, *Things Hidden: Scripture as Spirituality* (London: SPCK, 2016), 25. First published 2008.
4. Quoted in Richard Rohr, *Falling Upward* (San Francisco: Jossey Bass, 2011), 136.